Endorsements

Jonathan Larsen (Author, linguist, global storyteller)

Yoder's memoir takes the reader by the hand into a great gyre of a story beginning with an earthy Amish boyhood, to the forests of a First Nations settlement, to the thunder of Victoria Falls, to the sequoia of America's mountain west and to the Kansas prairies spread out before a college clock tower. That arc turns upon abiding questions: Who am I? and, Where do I belong? They lodge in his heart as Yoder gazes out upon the larger world from his early Shenandoah farm porch. His search for answers takes him into the world of books, across the globe during a career in higher learning, and now to this story.

Don Clymer (Writer, cross-cultural educator. Eastern Mennonite University faculty emeritus)

During one of his myriad moves, Yoder stated: "[I feel] somehow being nowhere in the middle of somewhere." From a shy but curious Amish boy to a high-level administrator at two Universities, Yoder crosses cultural boundaries that leave him almost always feeling outside looking in, "somehow being nowhere in the middle of somewhere." From Red Lake, Canada, to Botswana, Africa, Yoder paints beautiful pictures of his experiences and his thought processes in vivid and intriguing detail. This memoir really captures the interest of any reader who wants to understand intercultural relationships and knowledge. I highly recommend it.

David and Yvonne Freeman (Professors Emeriti, University of Texas Rio Grande Valley, Authors of *Between Worlds*)

John Yoder vividly describes how his experiences deeply shaped a life that took him in directions that were far from his childhood as an Amish boy in Kansas and Virginia. His adventures while working at a school in the northern Canadian wilderness were radically different from his teaching experiences at a university in Africa, and serving as a dean of a university in California was very different from being an administrator of a university in Kansas. Yoder reflects on how he has been "in" many different places but not necessarily "of" them and how his varied experiences have helped shape who he has become. These reflections invite readers to examine the influences that have shaped their own lives.

Ruth Keidel Clemens (Former International Program Director for Mennonite Central Committee)

John Yoder describes in great detail the life of an Amish boy growing into maturity and discovery of the broader world from a personal perspective. I felt like I was actually walking next to him through his experiences. His description of gaps in his collegiate knowledge due to growing up in isolation from traditional education helped me to understand my own gaps in understanding American society having grown up in Africa.

Saloma Miller Furlong (Author of *Liberating Lomie: Memoir of an Amish Childhood* and *Bonnet Strings: An Amish Woman's Ties to Two Worlds*)

John Yoder's life story reads like a true *Bildungsroman*. He leaves the community of his childhood to seek education and benefits academically, professionally, and in self-development. His (and his family's) adventurous spirit leads him to faraway lands, and then he eventually circles back to where he came. Along the way he acquires wisdom and insight, from which readers will benefit. Anyone who has ever felt torn between conflicting worlds or undecided at life's crossroads will be enriched by Yoder's story

Steven Nolt (Director of Young Center for Anabaptist and Pietist Studies, Elizabethtown College and Author of *A History of the Amish*)

In this remarkable memoir, psychologist and educator John Yoder explores the unexpected joys of an improbable life. Raised in an

Amish home, Yoder absorbed the separatist ideal of being "in the world but not of the world." That dynamic, it turned out, had far more relevance than he realized when he left home, at age 20, to take a teaching job in a northern Ontario school for Indigenous children, the first of many choices, challenges, and risks that marked the years to follow. Whether attending graduate school, working as a professor in Botswana, or serving as a university administrator in California and Kansas, Yoder found that he was often the outsider within, someone who occupied a position on the margins, offering a perspective that raised new questions, afforded special insight, and facilitated personal growth. *Between: An Amish Boy's Odyssey* tells Yoder's life journey, as he found, in each experience, both new horizons and fresh ways of seeing where he had once been.

Therese DesCamp (MDiv, PhD, minister and author of *Hands Like Roots*)

Running like a plumbline through John Yoder's engaging memoir is his long quest to live consciously with differences and questions. The reader is invited to accompany Yoder as he questions and explores the religious and cultural worlds—some given, some chosen—in which he has lived. Rather than rushing to shave off a part of himself in order to belong, we watch Yoder allow himself to be decentered, to notice that he no longer fits. This book speaks, like a clear-sighted friend, of the central task of adulthood: understanding where we belong, and living with the discomfort of loss. The wisdom and example found in John Yoder's book is a gift and a blessing to the reader.

Madelaine Fletcher (Writer, Former Marketing and Communications Director)

Between is a fascinating look at an unusual journey. Born in Kansas, John Yoder's life has taken him to many different worlds far from his Amish Kansas and Virginia roots. His story is about the varied worlds he lived in – from the Canadian wilderness and

Botswana to Central Valley, California and yes, Kansas again. The theme of being "of" a world or "in" a world is central to his memoir and it made me think of things differently. I recommend *Between* for the thoughtful approach John Yoder has taken in reflecting on his life, and the stories of the many places he's been and the worlds he's occupied.

Between

Between

An Amish Boy's Odyssey

John Yoder

SANTOS BOOKS

First Printing, 2025
Published by Santos Books, LLC, Elizabethtown, PA
ISBN: 7978992890723

Contents

To MaDonna, Rodney, Juliette, Avery, Wren, Karla, Daryl, Sarah, Alex, and Ben. Without your love, support, and encouragement, this book would not have happened. Your suggestions have made it a better book.

To my parents, Tobe and Saloma (Nisly) Yoder who believed in me.

Acknowledgments

Special thanks to Conrad, members of the Santos Authors' Group and the many others who have read early drafts of the manuscript. Your encouragement and feedback have been invaluable.

Preface

This is a book is of remembering—recalling those parts of my story that still feel fresh, as well as those that have become clouded by time. It is also about re-membering—finding those parts of my story that have been, for whatever reasons, dis-membered, and inviting them back into membership with the whole. I search for connections between the then and the now; between the parts and the whole; looking for the coherence of a through-line in the story. The book is about the stories and the worlds that shaped me and that, to borrow a phrase from Frederick Buechner,[1] I now carry on my back like the shell of a snail. They have become part of who I am. But I've lived in multiple worlds; worlds as different from each other as Northern Ontario is from Southern Africa or as California is from Kansas. Could I have been all of them? Maybe none of them? What does it mean to be "in" or "of" a world, anyway? This memoir, then, is an account of worlds and borders and of negotiating the spaces between them.

The story of one's life is, in the end, a personal creation. It is a tapestry woven from the threads of our lives and how we choose to interpret them. It is about which of our stories we decide—consciously or not—to include and which we will ignore or reject. The tapestries are woven from strands of "familial, social and cultural DNA" that, just as surely as biological DNA, are passed on, consciously or unconsciously, from one generation to the next. From these threads—spliced, incomplete, and tangled as they may be—we weave our sense of self and of our self-in-the-world. They are stories remembered and stories forgotten; stories remembered but left untold—all of them leaving their traces in the weaving. But where does a story begin? With an account of birth? An account of a beginning? Birth stories are always extensions of the stories that come before them: the stories of parents and grandparents, not to mention those of still earlier generations —the parents of those grandparents and their parents before them.

The story of my family, then, might begin in the lean and hard years of the Midwest during the depression of the 1930s and the Dust Bowl years that followed, when crops failed year after year and even the most resilient gave way to despair. But beginning the story there doesn't account for the story of how my parents and grandparents came to be there in the first place. Nor does it consider those curious twistings and turnings of what some would call fate, such as the story of my paternal great-grandfather Dan, who proposed marriage to a young woman named Fannie. When Fannie asked for time to think about it (she was barely 16), Dan's attention turned elsewhere. A few years later, Fannie married a different young Amishman, Eli, who, as it turned out, would become my maternal grandfather, and Fannie, rather than becoming my paternal great-grandmother, became my maternal grandmother instead.

Dan, for his part, would be widowed three times, burying each of his three wives, one after the other, in three different states before marrying the fourth, who would outlive him. While all of that could be told as stories in their own right, those stories of my grandfather and his family being left motherless multiple times are threads in the tapestry of my story. Recognized or not, these threads are woven into the fabric of my life where they've become one part—perhaps a small one—of what has made me who I am.

+++++++

Note: I write about the Amish as I experienced them, but my depictions are not meant to be universal nor to imply that all Amish and Amish communities are the same. While they share a common European origin and largely share general beliefs and practices, there is considerable variation among them. I write from my experience with the Amish in the community where I grew up. Experiences in other Amish communities are likely to differ.

++++++

[1]Buechner, F. (1977). *Telling the Truth: The Gospel as Tragedy, Comedy and Fairy Tale.* Harper One, p. 3.

Part I: Journey

When you are not clear on a destination,
You do well to remember whence you came.
- African Saying

All journeys begin somewhere, though the actual place and time of their beginning might be disputed. Did the journey begin at the point of departure or when the planning for it began? Or, what about the circumstances that prompted the planning? Perhaps that's the journey's true beginning. So it is with stories of a life; the place at which to begin the telling is an arbitrary one. I've chosen to begin this telling at a time that was pivotal in the trajectory of my life and that of our family. Later chapters pick up the story of my family of origin and of how growing up in an Amish family and community has shaped me. Then I back-fill the narrative with stories about origins, about how things came to be what they were. Each part of the collective narrative is important in order to understand the whole.

{ one }

Destination Botswana

Light rain spattered against the windows of our plane as it banked lazily into alignment with the runway, touched down, and rolled to a stop. A long journey had finally come to an end...or had it? We learned later of the old belief in semi-desert Botswana that they who arrive with rain[1] bring good fortune. Whether or not our arrival brought any good fortune to Botswana is an open question, but our arrival clearly marked, for us, a significant flexion point in our lives. We were a family of five; two parents, MaDonna and I, and our three children: Daryl, 9; Karla,11; and Rodney, 13. We had spent the last two nights inside the "transit hotel" at Jan Smuts Airport in the then-white-ruled South Africa. The transit hotel was where arrivals without South African visas or who were otherwise *persona non grata* were kept until they could arrange passage elsewhere.

The DC-3 had taken off from Jan Smuts International Airport[2] at Johannesburg, South Africa, about an hour earlier; then, rolling slightly north-west, headed for Gaborone (Ha-bor-o-ney), the capital city of Botswana. Barely two decades have passed since Gaborone—originally called Gaberones, after a tribal chieftain—had been little more than a stop on the Pretoria leg of the unfinished Cape-to-Cairo railroad. When Botswana, formerly the British protectorate of Bechuanaland, was granted independence in 1966, its leaders chose this village, less than 15 miles from the South African border, to become their nation's capital city. Now, after almost 20 years of both planned and unplanned development—and after dramatic in-migration from outlying areas of Botswana, as well as immigration from neighboring countries—the former village was now a national capital. But, as we would discover, the city and the country that we would call home for the next seven years could be both charmingly simple and confusingly complicated. And we loved it.

From the air, we had caught glimpses of a dusty landscape: long stretches of semi-arid grassland punctuated by native acacia trees; broken, here and there, with "kopjes" (rocky hillocks). Occasionally, we could make out a small village: a cluster of round one-room houses with a thatched roof or simple houses of concrete block with a cor-rugated tin roof, usually clustered around a standpipe or water tank that marked a well. Sometimes we could make out small herds of cattle or goats, usually with one or more small boys keeping watch nearby. As the plane banked and then settled onto the tarmac, the airport took shape: a single asphalt runway with a small huddle of white-painted buildings at one end, Botswana's national flag—light blue with black and white "zebra stripes" across the center—flutter-ing above them in the damp breeze.

A cluster of people stood along the edge of the runway watching the plane land. Emerging from the plane, we heard someone calling our names and waving at us. The man came up and introduced him-self as Fremont, director of Mennonite Ministries in Botswana—an affiliation of several humanitarian, mission, and educational pro-jects in the country. Though this was our first meeting, we felt as though we knew him. Fremont had been an invaluable contact and resource as we worked out the sometimes complicated details that made our arrival possible. Fremont had played an important role in the run-up to our decision to come to Botswana as well as, in the weeks leading up to our arrival, becoming an indispensable con-tact and communications channel with the University about prac-tical matters such as ticketing, living arrangements and getting our children enrolled into English Medium schools (schools where the medium of instruction was English). Fremont and his wife, Sarah, became personal friends and provided invaluable support as we tried to understand and navigate our way through this new world.

The University of Botswana, where I had been invited to teach, stood directly across the two-lane road that skirted the airport boundary. UB, as it was known, was a young institution that had been chartered barely ten years earlier when the then-regional university serving Swaziland and Botswana[3] had been dissolved and each country had formed its own national university. From the airport, we could see the campus: a group of unassuming gray or white plastered buildings with metal roofs, scattered across an expanse of scrub grasses and acacia trees. Splashes of brightly colored bougainvillea accented walkways between some of the buildings.

Our family's trek to Botswana had begun more than a year earlier when MaDonna and I had begun to explore seriously the possibility of an overseas experience for our family. I was, at the time, in my fourth year as Superintendent of a K-12, church-affiliated school near the small town of Belleville, in the lush farming country of Central Pennsylvania's Kishacoquillas Valley, known locally as Big Valley. Situated between Front Mountain to the east and Back Mountain a few miles to the west, Big Valley was a picturesque setting of well-kept farms and a few small towns and villages, mostly scattered along the two-lane highway that ran the length of the valley.

The previous year, I had signed a contract with the board of my school for a second 3-year term as superintendent, but as we moved into the school year, I had begun to feel increasingly confined and restless. Big Valley, despite the name, was a small place, physically as well as socially and culturally. The previous year, I had been invited by the dean at my alma mater, a small college in Virginia, to consider a vacant faculty position in their education department. I was interested but felt obligated to complete the contract I had just signed in Belleville, and told the college I could only accept the position if I could defer it for a year. They were, understandably, unwilling to wait and hired someone else. But even thinking about the possibility of leaving heightened what had been, for me, a growing sense that perhaps it was time to move on.

That also happened to be the fall that I had traveled with our high school faculty to a teacher's conference and retreat in the mountains of Western Pennsylvania. The featured speaker was a veteran educator and relief worker who had spent much of his career working and living in other countries. "Everyone should spend at least a year or two living abroad," he said, "you will never be the same." His argument was persuasive, but I couldn't see any way we could make it work for us. Travel was expensive, and MaDonna and I had three school-age children. We had trouble enough just keeping our bills paid on time. Maybe sometime later.

But over the next several months, I began, for the first time, to seriously wonder if we could find a way to make it work. But when and how? MaDonna and I agreed that the ideal time to do this would be while the children were still young enough to go with us and enjoy the experience. But traveling abroad as a family of five would stretch our budget beyond breaking. Still, I wondered, what if one could somehow do good on someone else's dime, so to speak. The idea became a chink in a window that we had, until then, assumed was closed. At the time, Canada and Mexico were the extent of either of our international travels. Still, my restlessness at the Belleville school began to be fed by a growing interest in traveling and perhaps living abroad—even if only for a short while. When we talked about it as a family, our kids thought living in another country would be a grand adventure!

Over the next several months, we began exploring possibilities; at first tentatively, then more seriously. We began conversations with international mission and service agencies. I subscribed to several newsletters that posted positions in universities and schools abroad and wrote letters of inquiry to several. Sometimes there was an acknowledgment in response, sometimes there was nothing. As time passed, several possibilities with different agencies began emerging: Thailand, Kenya, Papua New Guinea, but nothing was yet concrete, and conversations were ongoing.

Among the letters of inquiry I wrote was one to the University of Botswana, which had posted a notice in one of the newsletters for a two-year position teaching Educational Psychology in their Faculty of Education. The position was in my field, and I had written to the address given, but heard nothing in response. Nothing, that is, until one day in mid-March, we found a fat, special delivery envelope in our mailbox with a return address from the University of Botswana in Gaborone. The envelope contained an offer and a contract for a two-year teaching appointment with the possibility of renewal. The salary was stated in Botswana's national currency, the Pula. The accompanying letter said that if I accepted their offer, I should return the contract at my earliest convenience and, further, that the assignment would commence on July 1st.

This was mid-March, and at school, we were already busy wrapping up the year; there was simply no way, we thought, that we could accept their offer. We couldn't break up our household, make travel arrangements, say our farewells in Pennsylvania as well as in our parental homes in Virginia and Oregon, respectively, and be in Botswana in three months! I was still under contract to the Board of my school for another year, and, anyway, we had begun to have second thoughts about the wisdom of taking our three children out of the American school system with no assurance of what would come next. (Even though the children themselves thought it would be a lark!) Then there were questions about the salary. The salary offered by the University of Botswana, converted to US dollars, was less than what we had been living on, and it wasn't at all clear that it would support a family of five for two years, even in Botswana, where the cost of living would be lower. My cautious Amish mind shrank back, it was a risk we couldn't take.

But then we began having second thoughts about our second thoughts. Maybe this was the opportunity we'd been looking for. Would an opportunity like this ever come by again? What if, maybe, just maybe, we could make this work? Thus began a flurry of communication with people who were in positions to answer some of our questions. Someone had given us Fremont's contact information in Botswana. We began communicating directly with him, and he, in turn, connected us with others who encouraged us to dig deeper. Soon, a sense of optimism began to emerge. Maybe we could make this work! After some telexed[4] exchanges directly with the University it was agreed, for one thing, that I could delay beginning the contract until September. The University would pay for our family's travel expenses, provide subsidized housing, and seemed hopeful that our children could find places in schools where English was the medium of instruction.[5]

It wasn't an easy or instant decision, but in the end, we decided to take the risk; I returned the signed contract by special handling, and the die was cast. The children were excited. I immediately tendered a letter to my school board, asking to be released from the final year of my three-year contract. They reluctantly but graciously agreed. In hindsight, we thought little about what we would do or where we would live when we returned to the States. In what must have been a burst of unjustified hubris, we apparently assumed that things would somehow work out.

The decision to leave for Botswana by the end of the summer triggered a whirlwind of activity: selling our house, deciding what of our stuff we should take along, what was important enough to store, and where. (In the end, it was surprising to see how much stuff we decided was not worth keeping!) Friends offered to store a few pieces of furniture and some boxes. The university would pay for our travel, but it would only include the airlines' regular baggage allowances for international travel: one carry-on bag and two checked bags each. A checked bag, we learned, could be a small trunk provided it fell within the airline's weight and dimension limits. But all of the things we thought we would need for the next two years: clothes, personal items, even basic kitchen ware (we had been told that some items we thought of as basic might be hard to find in Botswana) had to fit into the five small trunks and five bags we would be able to check!

By the end of July, we had managed to sell our house, dispose of disposables, store a few things, take a carload of things to my parents' place in Virginia, pack five bags and five small trunks and buy Amtrak tickets that would take us from Virginia to Portland, Oregon. The University of Botswana promised that we would have the needed travel authorizations and airline tickets from Portland to Gaborone for our departure in August. Our route would take us from Portland—via Los Angeles, London, and Johannesburg (with a refueling stop in Cape Verde)—on our way to Gaborone.

Crossing the continent from Virginia to Oregon by train through Chicago, Denver, and San Francisco was long but scenic and relaxing. We were wowed by the changing views from the dome car, where we spent much of our time from Chicago onward. Three days cloistered on a train also offered time for reflection and book-ended the transition we had undertaken. No doubt more than we may have realized, the days on the train, traveling from one coast to the other, were a kind of symbolic journey, epitomizing what we were about to do: travel from one world into another. It was the beginning of a journey that—both literally and figuratively—would take us to the other side of the world. Portland and the nearby community of Estacada, where MaDonna had grown up, where we had been married, and where her parents and siblings still lived, were familiar territory, of course. Still, our focus had now shifted to things beyond.

When we got to Estacada, though, our most immediate concerns were establishing a firm date for departure and having the airline tickets and necessary visas in hand. After we had agreed on the revised start date for my teaching assignment, the University was to authorize a work permit and purchase tickets for our family. In order to meet the deadline for the beginning of my teaching contract, we would need to arrive in Gaborone in late August. The flights from Portland to Johannesburg were, as we discovered, relatively straightforward, but the final leg—from Johannesburg to Gaborone—was more complicated. The only flights departing to Botswana from the Jan Smuts Airport[6] were on Botswana's national airline: Air Botswana. But Air Botswana did not participate in the international airline reservation system at the time, so it was impossible to make advance reservations for the final leg of our trip. We would have to be in South Africa in order to get tickets for our flight to Botswana. The government of white-ruled South Africa had been mired in the struggle with what they considered anti-government forces for years and was hypersensitive to anyone or anything that might, even remotely, pose a security risk. Their visa rules were strict; we would need visas, even if only for one night.

Accordingly, early in the summer, well before our departure dates, we had obtained American passports and mailed visa applications, with the supporting documentation, to the South African Embassy in Washington, DC. The visas, they assured us by phone, would not be a problem, and, after discussing options for getting the visas physically stamped into our passports, we agreed that it could be done at their consulate in Los Angeles on our way through, as we would have several hours of layover there. There would be time enough for me to take our passports to the consular office in Los Angeles, where the visas could be stamped in. This seemed a bit risky to me, but not knowing any better options, we agreed. The South African Consulate in Los Angeles was only about 30 minutes by cab from the airport. There should be plenty of time if flights were on time and everything functioned according to plan. We expected to be in Portland for about a week before flying out. The University would purchase the tickets and make the flight arrangements. In addition to several hours layover in Los Angeles, we would have most of a day in London before transferring to South African Airways[7] for our flight to Johannesburg. We were instructed to check with the airlines to verify the reservations and to claim our tickets.

Days went by, but no ticket. As our departure date drew near, our anxiety mounted, and we began to wonder if this had all been a bad idea, that the University of Botswana couldn't be trusted, or that the job offer wasn't real. In some desperation, we eventually made contact by phone with Fremont in Botswana, who offered to go to the University on our behalf. In a return phone call a few days later, Fremont relayed an apology from UB and gave us a new date for departure and when the tickets should be expected. To our great relief, this time they arrived.[8]

Our family of five must have attracted more than one glance as we waited at the United Airlines check-in counter. Each of us carried a carry-on bag (no laptops in those days) and two checked bags, including the small trunk—ten bags in all—stacked on carts, needing to be checked in. The check-in process bogged down when the counter personnel discovered that we were flying to South Africa without visas. It took some discussion and explaining about arrangements for getting the promised visas in Los Angeles before boarding passes were issued, but only to Los Angeles.

Arriving in Los Angeles, I dashed out to hail the nearest cab to the South African Consulate. When I arrived, the consular officials seemed to be expecting me. They took the five passports and disappeared into a back room while I kept my eyes on the clock. After what seemed an eternity, a different official appeared with the passports. Handing them back, he said, "I'm sorry, but we can't give you visas at this time."

At first, I wasn't sure I had heard him right. We had gotten verbal approval from officials in Washington; didn't that matter? We couldn't make arrangements to leave South Africa until we had entered South Africa, but we couldn't enter South Africa because we had no arrangements in place to leave! But any attempts to explain or ask for reasons were met with the same polite: "I'm sorry, but there's nothing more we can tell you." In the end, there was nothing to do but return to the airport, visa-less passports in hand. Now our entire itinerary was in doubt. But, having no other options, there wasn't much to do but proceed.[9]

Because this was an international flight, passports and visas were being re-checked at the gate in Los Angeles. We tried to appear nonchalant and as inconspicuous as possible. But no such luck. When we got to the gate, we were pulled out of line and told we couldn't board because we had no South African visas or confirmed flights out. The gate agents' response was, at first, adamant: we couldn't board. But after more explanation, showing them my teaching contract and work permit for Botswana, the agents (a supervisor had arrived by this time) looked at each other and waved us on; deciding, no doubt, that it was easier to leave us to our fates than to figure out what to do with a family of five underway to some place in Africa. One of the gate agents mentioned something about a transit hotel at South Africa's Jan Smuts airport, but he seemed uncertain about it.

Arriving at Jan Smuts International Airport after our day[10] in London followed by a long night flight (with a refueling stop in Cape Verde), we were unprepared for the military vehicles that pulled up next to our plane as it taxied to a stop, nor for the armed soldiers scrutinizing our faces and our movements as we disembarked and walked over to the busses that would take us to the terminal. (I remember especially noticing one of the young soldiers, barely old enough to have finished secondary school. He had a kind of pleasant appearance despite all of the military gear he was carrying. I wondered how he felt about the job he had been assigned to do. He could have been a next-door neighbor's son.) This was our introduction to South Africa. We had known of the ongoing struggle for Black majority rule in South Africa, but now it felt uncomfortably real.

We learned at the Air Botswana desk that the first possible flight to Gaborone would be mid-morning the next day. Still, the desk agent said it was unlikely that we could get seats on it because there was a contingent of American Peace Corps workers also wanting to get to Gaborone. It seemed that the Peace Corps workers would have first rights to those seats. But he told us to come back to the gate in the morning to check. Meanwhile, South African security personnel stood by to escort us to the transit hotel, where we were secured in two modest hotel rooms. The official pointed out a restaurant next door (also secured) where we could eat if we chose to. The Peace Corps workers, it turned out, did take up all the available seats on the next day's flight, and we spent a second night in detention. Seats opened up for us the next day, and we were put aboard an elderly, twin-engine DC-3, the then-workhorse of the Air Botswana fleet, and were soon airborne.

Our family couldn't have realized, at that time, the extent to which our on-again-off-again journey from Central Pennsylvania and Oregon to Southern Africa symbolized a passage between worlds; how our stay in Africa would become a flexion point—a hinge point—that would change our lives, our sense of ourselves and our ways of seeing the world. I could not have known, then, how the University of Botswana and my colleagues there would become my intellectual and academic home for seven years. How that coming to know them as friends and colleagues, and learning something of their life stories and the worlds they represented, would challenge me to examine and see my own in a new and different light.

Instead of being an interesting two-year interlude, our years in Botswana would deflect the overarching trajectory of our lives. Before actually getting there, we had, without overmuch thought, considered the opportunity to spend two years in Africa as a way of serving others and of seeing a different part of the world, after which we would return to our own country and more or less pick up from where we had left off. But that's not what happened. Instead, our years in Africa turned our views of ourselves and of the world inside-out. Far more than an interesting couple of years, our years in Botswana became a kind of reset; a renegotiation of how we saw and understood ourselves and the world we lived in. We had crossed cultural borders and became participants in worlds we had hardly imagined.

No longer mostly among our own kind, the concept of "other" would take on new meaning as we discovered that it was we, white privileged Americans with a particular point of view, who were the ones on the margins and not the other way around. We would be perplexed by something that, for want of a better word might be called fate, in which the narrative of the families and cultures into which we are born—through no choice of our own—become the norm, the core narrative—religious, secular or both, by which we define and defend our ways of seeing, believing and behaving in the world and how that becomes the basis by which we judge others.

++++++

[1] Rain is important in drought-prone, semi-desert Botswana. The name of their national currency, *Pula*, is also the word for rain and for blessing.

[2] Now, O.R. Tambo International Airport

[3] Which had still earlier included Basutoland (later Lesotho), Bechuanaland (later Botswana), and Swaziland: UBBS. Following Lesotho's independence, it became UBLS.[4] This was before email and texting! Telexes were a somewhat less expensive form of sending something like a telegram.

[5] The government elementary schools taught in the local language. Places in English-medium schools were in short supply due to the high demand for children of diplomatic corps members and other foreign nationals, including university professors from abroad.

[6] Following the transition to Black rule, the airport was renamed; first Johannesburg International Airport and later the O.R. Tambo International Airport, in honor of the anti-apartheid politician, Oliver Tambo.

[7] Due to sanctions placed on South Africa by many of the world's countries and corporations protesting apartheid, South African Airways did not have the right to fly overland across any African countries. So, after leaving England, the flight path paralleled the west coast of Africa but over international waters, with a refueling stop in Cape Verde.

[8] The Tickets were with United Airlines, which was apparently the only American carrier still flying to South Africa at the time.

[9] It was only later, after being denied visas twice more after arrival in Botswana, that we began to suspect the reasons for the South African authorities' unwillingness to grant us visas. Some years before, an American volunteer, John Howard Yoder (same middle initial as mine), had drawn attention from the South African authorities for his anti-apartheid activities and was declared *persona non grata*. It was only after I convinced the authorities that I was a different John H. Yoder that our family was issued South African visas. Over the years, we have traveled in South Africa numerous times for various reasons. It's a beautiful country!

[10]Green-horns that we were, we left the airport to "see the city" during our day-long layover in London, but sleep deprivation had taken its toll by that time, and none of us remembers much of it.

Part II: Roots

**We are dropped into a socially constructed world created by
people who are now long dead.
- Paraphrase from Peter Berger**

We construct our world, and then we live in it. It's a mental construct, of course, but we build it out of the raw material of experience and, most importantly, from our interpretation of the
experience. But the life-narrative we construct; our story and our interpretation of it, is shaped in part—often below our awareness—by
the strands of the narratives that we've inherited. Those stories,
sometimes reaching back for generations, have been woven willy-
nilly into the familial, the social and the cultural DNA we've inherited from our parents—and they from their parents and so on ad
infinitum.

The choice of where to begin a story is always an arbitrary one
because every story presupposes a still earlier one. I begin this telling
of my story in Kansas, the state and the place of my birth and that
of my parents before me. The stories of my parents, grandparents,
and great-grandparents and of the land and the people in which
their stories are situated were woven into their life-narratives and,
through them, into mine.

The chapters in Part Two are arranged in a non-linear sequence.
I begin with a chapter on Kansas and follow it with a chapter telling
the story of my family's move halfway across the continent to Virginia, where I grew up. The story then pivots back in to an earlier time, with a chapter that picks up the stories that my parents,
grandparents and great-grandparents lived and told. Their stories,
and their manner of telling them, became the stories of my parents,

and they have in turn shaped the self-narratives that we, their children and grandchildren, tell ourselves about who we are and why.

{ two }

Kansas

I was born into an Amish home in rural Eastern Kansas, near the small town of Garnett in Anderson County. It was during the early hours of a Saturday morning, on November 13th. The year was 1943. Franklin Roosevelt was president, and World War II would rage on for almost two more years before being brought to an end by an unthinkable force from high above Hiroshima and Nagasaki. The years of both the Depression and the Midwest's Dust Bowl were still painfully recent in that part of the country. In that part of the United States, there were few signs of the economic recovery that would come in the decades after the end of the War.

Southeastern Kansas has been (and still is) something of a hardscrabble region. My parents moved there—to Garnett, the county seat of Anderson County—when the small Amish community near Nowata, in Northeastern Oklahoma, had broken up after the death of its founder, my grandfather, Eli Nisly. That was the community where my parents had met, been married, and where the first four of their six children were born. I was the first and only one of my siblings to be born in Garnett and in a hospital[1]—such as it was. More a clinic and doctor's office than a hospital, it was housed in a square, two-story brick building a few blocks from Courthouse Square with the Anderson County Courthouse at its center.

I have only the faintest of memories, if that is what they are, of those early years in Kansas. My parents had somehow managed to buy a small farm, three miles due west of town. My older siblings describe our house, the one where I lived for most of my three years, as a small, one-and-a-half-story farmhouse with clapboard siding, typical of Kansas farmhouses of the time. The house was shaped like a T, with the second story consisting of only two rooms above the stem of the T. The ceilings sloped on both sides because of the roof. A narrow stairway in the corner of the middle room downstairs led to the upstairs rooms. I have a faint memory of being in a bed that was shoved against a wall with the ceiling sloping down when I was sick with measles. Other vague, impressionistic memories involve being outside, seated in a toy wagon, and being upset by the nearby chickens.

Water was carried in from the well in the backyard with a hand pump, and kerosene lanterns or gas-powered pressure lamps provided light. Several large trees—one of them remembered to be a mulberry—shaded the farm yard and one side of the house. The pasture for the livestock was located beyond the barn and included a small woodlot. My school-age older siblings could cut across a field to walk a quarter mile to the one-room schoolhouse at the crossroads, just a quarter mile from our farm lane. A large oak tree shaded the school yard.

In moving from Oklahoma to Kansas, my father exchanged the horses he used for the field work for a steel-wheeled Farmall tractor that had to be started using a hand crank. Horses were still kept for some farm tasks and for pulling the buggy to church on Sunday or for making a trip to town. My brother Leo, who would have been about 10 or 11 years old at the time, tells of being put aboard the slow-moving tractor, guiding it across the field while pulling a plow or a harrow. His feet couldn't reach the pedals from the tractor seat so he had to stand in order to work the clutch pedal. He was particularly proud of the time when he was able to start the engine using the hand crank. (That only worked when the engine was cold, he said. When the engine was warm, it didn't start as easily, and he had to call on Dad to start it.)

We were, in most respects, I think, a typical Amish farm family. Mom, short (well under five feet), always on the move, a lover of birds, flowers, gardening, and the out-of-doors, was the "executive director" of many areas of our family life. Dad was usually content to follow her lead, although it was clear that major decisions were made jointly, often out of earshot of us children. They led a quiet lifestyle and a faith that was more evident in their daily living than in words.

My parents followed the understood division of labor among the Amish (and many non-Amish, for that matter). Dad did the heavy farm work: raising and harvesting crops, tending the animals, building and repairing fences, keeping the farmstead in working order, often working long hours in the hot sun. Mom was in charge of housekeeping, food preparation and preservation, and managing the vegetable garden, assisted, of course, by us children as we became old enough to help. She also managed the chickens, took care of the eggs, and sometimes did the evening milking if Dad was tied up with other work, milking 2 or 3 cows by hand into a metal bucket. Generally, men's work was outdoor work; women's work was mostly indoor work, except for the vegetable garden and the chickens. It was an understood, though largely unspoken, partnership and division of labor with both parents working within their own spheres to keep their family and their farm together and afloat.

In our own way, we siblings were close, though generally not very demonstrative; touching, hugging, and verbal expressions of love were not part of our inherited social DNA. But we believed in each other and, generally, in ourselves. It was much later that I realized the extent to which this could be attributed to our parents' confidence in us at an early age. They trusted and believed in us, and we mostly lived up to their expectations. This realization became clearer as we grew older. After we moved to Virginia (described in a later section) and Leo left home, I was, for example, essentially treated as an adult and given adult responsibilities after I left school at the age of 16. Leo was still young when, at the age of 13 or 14, he was given the responsibility to design and then build the system of underground water pipes — digging the ditches by hand — that would distribute water from the then-new public water supply to strategic points around our little farm. (Dad was working outside of the home at the time and couldn't take time off from work.) It was a pattern that was repeated with all of us to varying degrees. We came to believe, through our parents' actions more than by their words, that we were competent and capable and could be trusted with almost anything if we put our minds to it. Though impossible to measure, there's no doubt that their confidence in us played an important role in the choices we would make in later life.[2]

Sundays were rigorously observed as a day of rest and for attending church. Besides cooking the Sunday meals and washing the dishes, the only permitted work was the necessary care and feeding of the animals. Some families did not allow their children to even play quiet games on Sunday afternoons, let alone anything vigorous, such as a ball game. (Our family was not quite that strict, but followed similar principles. We could read or play quiet games, but nothing noisy or active.)

Sunday services were held in the homes of church members, rotating systematically from one family to another on a weekly basis. The services might last 2-3 hours. In addition to singing German hymns, there were typically two sermons, delivered extemporaneously in the everyday language of the Amish, Pennsylvania Dutch.[3] The Bible, though, was read from Martin Luther's 16th-century German translation. After the service, a simple meal, served on the same backless benches on which they had been sitting during the service, offered a time for visiting and catching up with each other, before the horses were hitched back to the buggies for the trip home to do the evening chores. The meal typically consisted of bread—home-baked, of course—and condiments such as apple butter and pickled beets—a favorite of mine, I'm told—and coffee. Sometimes there was a milk soup with beans and bread. (I'm still fond of pickled beets, and the smell of percolating coffee can bring up something vague and hazy that feels like a memory.)

This was the family, the community, and the world into which I was born and into which I began to be socialized long before I had any awareness of it. It was a community that, like all Amish communities, drew a bright line between "us" and "them"—the Amish and the non-Amish or "English." Though they lived in the world with the non-Amish, the Amish were not of it. Their distinctive religious beliefs and practices, their social structures, and their deeply ingrained lifestyle, reinforced by strong family and kinship ties, kept the boundaries clear. The non-Amish were different; their lifestyle, the Amish believed, was dictated by worldly ways, and the lines dividing the two were clear: their clothing and hairstyles were distinct; their houses were furnished more simply, and they drove horses and buggies instead of cars and trucks. But there was also a mindset, an internal sense of being different and apart, that was subtle and harder to describe, but nevertheless part of what it meant to be Amish. For most members of the Amish community, having been socialized inside those closely guarded boundaries meant there was rarely an occasion—overtly at least—to question the assumptions and worldview of their birth community; all was woven into a seamless fabric.

Some seventy years later, my siblings and I visited the old farmstead during a family reunion in a nearby state park. The old lane leading into what had been our farm was overgrown and impassible, nearly hiding the faded No Trespassing sign hanging crookedly from a wire across the entrance. But we made our way through an adjacent field to the old farmstead. Only a jumble of crumbling foundation stones, along with some mangled pipes and the rusty remains of a child's toy wagon, marked the spot where the house had once stood. A depression in the yard showed the spot where the storm cellar had collapsed onto itself. There was no sign of the barn, though there was an open space where Leo believed it had once been. Weathered and leaning crazily, a small shed still stood as it must have been seventy years before. Being there and recreating in my mind's eye the place as it used to be (or was it retrieving some nascent half-formed memory from my then-two-year-old brain?) triggered a kind of deja vu—a feeling of having been there before—that was hard to explain. Perhaps it was tricks of memory or something deeper and less well understood, but it seemed clear that this long-ago place of family beginnings had somehow left its mark on us.

++++++

[1] My mother tells of being taken to the "hospital" when she was in labor with me and being told that all the beds were full; there was no room for her. As she tells it, it was only after she insisted that a bed was made available for her by moving someone else into the hallway.

[2] Our family was unusual among the Amish in that five of us six, went on to advanced training or education: three of my sisters completed nurses' training (while remaining Amish), Leo became a physician and a recognized expert in Hanson's Disease (leprosy); once testifying before a congressional committee. I earned a Ph.D. and had a career in higher education.

[3] Pennsylvania Dutch is generally the Amish's everyday spoken language, but Amish children were taught to read High German. Many children acquired English as a second language before entering school, but some only became fluent after starting school.

{ three }

Stuarts Draft

Three years after the Yoder clan had moved to Kansas from the Amish community in Oklahoma (described later), my uncle Ben and his family moved again; this time half-way across the continent to a small Amish community in Virginia, near the country town of Stuarts Draft. It wasn't long after they had moved to Garnett that Uncle Ben and Aunt Mary and the other members of the Yoder-Nisly clan had begun to be unhappy with the Amish community there. They were especially concerned that their children would be influenced by what they saw as a wild streak among the Amish youth there, some of whom were known to drink and party. At the invitation of Uncle Ed, who had moved east some years earlier, Ben and Mary made an exploratory visit to the relatively new Amish community near Stuarts Draft. They returned to Kansas with glowing reports of what they had found and made the decision to move there.

By early the following year (with financial help from Uncle Ed (who had done well on the sale of property in Virginia's Tidewater region), Ben and Mary had bought a farm near Stuarts Draft. The Amish in Stuarts Draft were "Church Amish," slightly more progressive than the Kansas Amish in some details—they allowed electricity in their houses and on their farms, for example, and rubber tires on their tractors—but in most ways, they followed the same Amish practices and beliefs. The Virginia farmland was rich, and the climate was conducive to crop growth. Ben and Mary reported that the young people respected the church and were well-behaved.

My parents were especially close to Ben and Mary and decided, never having set foot in Virginia, to follow them there. In the fall of 1946, my parents sold their Kansas farm, including the land, livestock, farming equipment, and most of their household goods. They then created up the few things they could afford to take along and boarded a train that would take their family and their belongings halfway across the country into a different—but—still Amish world.

The land, farming practices, and cultural environment in Virginia could hardly have been more different from those in Kansas. And, though it wasn't talked about in polite company, everyone knew that within the Stuarts Draft Amish community, there were major economic differences between the first Amish to settle in Stuarts Draft and those who came later. The first Amish who moved to the area in the early '40s were from Virginia's Tidewater region and came as economic refugees of a sort—but not because they were poor. Quite the opposite. When, in the years leading up to and during World War II, the rural lifestyle of the Amish had become progressively untenable, they chose to leave. The roads had become crowded and unsafe for the horses and buggies of the Amish, and land prices had skyrocketed. Some of the Amish chose to stay and became part of a more liberal group that permitted cars. But others sold their farms and businesses to the military or to developers—apparently for a healthy profit—and moved away.

The Amish from the Tidewater region came to Stuarts Draft with money in their pockets, which they used to buy up choice farms and properties. This was not so true for the Amish who came later from other parts of the country, notably among them, the Yoders from Kansas, who came with precious few resources. Fortunately for the Yoders, there was, in fact, a rich uncle (by marriage[11]) who was also inclined to be generous. Uncle Ed had moved East years earlier and had apparently done quite well with the sale of property in the Tidewater region before moving to Stuarts Draft with the other Amish. He provided the financing for Uncle Ben to purchase his farm and for my parents to buy their place along Route 12. He held the notes for many years.

But despite origin or wealth, there was a commonality of spirit and vocabulary among the Amish. They shared a worldview and a plethora of cultural traditions that didn't need to be negotiated or explained. They understood each other. Though they might differ in some details of Amish culture and some points of expression, each had a deep and shared understanding of what it meant to be Amish. It was, in many ways, a shared faith, culture, and worldview that could be traced in an almost straight line to its roots in rural Switzerland more than 300[2] years earlier. Besides matters of faith and belief, there were, for example, cultural practices—sometimes elevated to religious belief—such as a prohibition against having buttons on men's coats. The Amish required "hooks and eyes" instead. Sometimes there were differences between the practices we Western Amish brought with us and those of the East Coast Amish[3] (the founders) but the Westerners—as far as I could tell, usually accepted the Easterners' practices without overt resistance. Though my parents were not likely to talk much for or against specific church practices, there were times when it was clear that they would have preferred the lines to be drawn differently.

Before we arrived in Virginia, Uncle Ben had made arrangements for Dad to work for an Amish farmer who also happened to have a tenant house[4] on his farm into which we could move. While it sounded like a good arrangement, the reality turned out to be an unhappy one from the beginning. Mom had been expecting a house that was at least up to the standards of our simple Kansas farmhouse, but knowing the new *ordnung* (church rules) they'd be living under, was also looking forward to perhaps having electricity and running water in the house—maybe even an indoor bathroom—none of which would have been allowed at the time by the Kansas Amish. So it is easy to imagine her disappointment when they were shown the house. The driveway, a farm lane, actually, led through a cow pasture and curved up a steep hill for some distance. The view of the valley with the Blue Ridge mountains in the background was great, but the house was a disappointment. It was an old wood-frame structure whose better days were long gone. The wooden siding hadn't seen a paint brush in years, the floors sagged, there were cracks around the windows, and, worst of all from Mom's point of view, there were mice! Lots of them! Water had to be carried to the house from a cistern outside, and the nearest electrical line was a half-mile away along the highway. The job Dad was to have did not work out well either; Dad found the farmer, though a fellow Amishman, to be hard to please. Up until the move to Virginia, of course, Dad had owned his own farm and had been his own boss. So it didn't take long before my parents began looking for other options.

Within a few months, Mom and Dad found a place along Route 12 (now US 340) that they were able to buy (with the financial backing from Uncle Ed). Our new home was a kind of mini-farm of two and a half acres about a mile west of the intersection where State Route 608 crossed Route 12. There was a small, red-brick house with three bedrooms and—an amazing luxury for a family recently arrived from rural Kansas—an indoor bathroom! Besides the house, there were two broiler houses (sheds for growing broiler chickens), a small barn, and a pasture where we could keep our horse and a cow. There were fruit trees and a large garden for growing vegetables. And there was a roomy garage which, though obviously built for automobiles, would do quite well for a buggy!

Our house, small by current standards, was, to our rural Kansas Amish eyes, stunningly modern. Not only was there indoor plumbing, but there was electricity throughout and lights that could be turned on or off by the flick of a switch! No more lighting kerosene or gas lamps every evening! (Even the farmhouse that Uncle Ben's family had moved into didn't have that! They did add it later, though.) Mom remarked later that she felt a bit guilty about living in such luxury. This would be our family home for the next twenty years.

The town of Stuarts Draft—scarcely more than a village at that time—boasted a post office and a smattering of stores along its Main Street: a drug store, a couple of hardware stores, a feed store, a bank and, a little further north along Main Street, the public elementary school. The more well-to-do citizens who chose to live in town had built large houses along both sides of Main Street north of the business district. The Norfolk and Western Railroad maintained a freight and passenger service at a small depot on the South end of Main Street. I well remember lying in bed and hearing the distant, long, and somehow lonesome whistle of the steam locomotives as they passed during the night.

Stuarts Draft was, at the time, an agricultural community[5] in more or less the central part of the southern Shenandoah Valley. Situated between the Blue Ridge mountains a few miles to the south and east and the Allegheny mountains several miles to the west, the valley was a rich agricultural area with apple orchards, dairy farms and large poultry operations. Before the arrival of Europeans, the area had been the territory of the Shawnee people, though also frequented by the Delaware and Catawba. In 1736, Virginia's then-governor, William Gooch, granted a patent for over 118,000 acres in Virginia to one William Beverly, who proceeded, over time, to sell off parcels. One of the early takers was Archibald Stuart, a Scottish Presbyterian, who later sold 353 acres of his property along the South River to his son Thomas. Thomas Stuart's property was said to have had a small valley or "cove" as locals called it, that was known regionally as a "draft;" thus the property became "Stuarts Draft."[6]

Some of the early European settlers in the area were German-speaking immigrants or were Pennsylvania-born children of German immigrants. But another group of the early settlers found their way into the foothills and mountains west and south of town, from the Appalachians to the south. Many were of Scotch-Irish descent, with surnames like Fitzgerald and Fretwell. The German-speaking immigrants and their descendants tended to be farmers, tradespeople or small business owners, settling onto agricultural land where small towns would soon grow up around them. The Scotch-Irish, on the other hand, who tended to be less well off, more often settled on less expensive land in the foothills and hollers (hollows) of the nearby mountains where they could clear land, raise their own vegetables, and keep a few animals for milk and meat. The mountain folk were independent people who tended to mind their own business, were generous and always willing to help each other, but were sometimes suspicious of outsiders.

Though the Amish who came to explore possibilities for settling around Stuarts Draft in 1930s and early 1940s,[7] must have caused some bemused head-scratching among the English, (a common term used by the Amish in reference to the non-Amish) the Amish came to be respected as good, hard-working and honest neighbors. Similarly, the Amish came to know their non-Amish neighbors as good people for the most part, despite their being outsiders. The Amish readily engaged their non-Amish neighbors in conversation and neighborly exchanges of tools or labor, but they almost always drew the line at purely social interaction. It would have been highly unusual, for example, for an Amish family to invite a non-Amish family into their home for a meal, or vice versa. It was clear that the Amish in Stuarts Draft, like Amish elsewhere, though living next door to non-Amish neighbors, nevertheless understood themselves to be living in a different world.

Situated within a few miles of the foothills in one direction and farms and farmland in the other, Stuarts Draft stood at a kind of cultural crossroads between the Appalachian culture to the west and south and the Germanic farm and small-town culture to the east and north. The distinctions between the cultures were rarely spoken of but recognized and understood; the lines between them usually remained clear. The Amish of Stuarts Draft, of course, saw themselves as "in but not of" those surrounding cultures.

Without our having realized, our two and half acre farm, only a few miles from town, was also located more or less at this confluence of cultures. On the valley floor and along its creeks were prosperous farms with spacious barns and stately farm houses (some of which were purchased by the Amish), while along the winding roads leading into the foothills and mountains were modest houses and smallholdings where the owners could raise vegetables and keep a few animals.

When we first moved to the house on Route 12, there were three filling stations within sight of our front porch. They were small general stores that sold a few basic groceries and pumped gasoline. They were also gathering places for regulars from around the area—the majority of whom would be from the nearby foothills—who would stop in after work or on weekends to hang out or play on pinball machines. Occasionally, there would be an impromptu jam session of mountain or bluegrass music, complete with fiddles, banjos, and guitars. We would watch and listen from our front porch, fascinated. There was no question, of course, of our being allowed to join them, but we had ring-side seats. Sometimes, when the weather was cold, we were allowed to wait for the school bus inside one of the filling stations. Though the filling stations would gradually disappear over the years, they offered us Amish children a wide-eyed window into language, cultures, and lifestyles that were completely different from anything I had known. I would try to imagine what it might be like to live as one of them.

We came to know the proprietors and many of their regulars by both name and reputation: they were truck drivers, loggers, and factory workers, still reflecting, in many ways, the mountain culture of the southern Appalachians. Among them were a few families that "everyone" understood to be "bootleggers"—making and selling illegal whiskey from a still hidden somewhere in a mountain holler (hollow). Though their names and their reputation were generally known, we never heard of any of their operations being "busted" by authorities. But the thought-to-be-bootleggers, like the others around them, were generally good neighbors and were more than ready to help anyone who needed it. Dad rented some mountain farmland from one of the "bootlegger families" for several years.

There was also another cultural stream to which I and, I suspect, most of our Amish community gave little thought: the African Americans. Many of these had deep roots in the area dating from before the Civil War. Virginia, like the rest of the South, was at the time strictly segregated. Public toilets, public drinking fountains, and restaurants—at least those that served African Americans—had separate entrances and facilities, as well as designated seating areas, labeled accordingly. Two different school buses passed our house on Route 12 when schools were in session: one carrying the white students to the large consolidated county high school and the other carrying the black students to a different one. I knew where the white high school was located (though no Amish kids would ever attend there), but even today, I have no idea where the school for Blacks was located. We knew a few African Americans who lived nearby; mostly elderly and living in substandard housing. There must have been other, younger, more well-to-do families living nearby, but I have no idea of where that would have been.

On occasion, my father (who by then was renting a neighboring farm) or other Amish farmers would hire one or two local Blacks when they needed someone to fill out a threshing crew.[8] I don't believe they were treated any differently or paid differently than others on the crew, but when it came time for dinner (as the mid-day meal was called) the Black workers would typically choose not to join the others around the table, asking instead to be served at a separate table apart from them. I can remember Mom encouraging one such worker to join the rest of the crew at the main table, but he demurred, preferring to eat by himself at a table on the back porch. The lines were clear; blacks, like the Amish, lived in a different world. They, too, were in the world of the dominant cultures, but they were not of it.

We could watch all of these slices of differentness—valley, foothills, Blacks—from our front porch, and I was fascinated. But my keen awareness of being different, along with my natural shyness, always colored my interactions with that outside world. Sometimes I tried to imagine what it must be like to live in their world. But mostly I just watched, as though from the opposite side of a window that couldn't be opened. I could only see through it.

As I grew older, though I wouldn't have been able to articulate it that way, I not only felt marginalized from the surrounding majority cultures, but began to feel a kind of reverse marginalization from the Amish culture as well. The more I knew of and imagined life outside of the Amish boundaries, the more marginalized I felt from the Amish world in which I was embedded. It was a kind of ironic reversal: while I was clearly and obviously in the Amish world, I was not fully in my head, at least, of it either. Externally, I generally complied with the cultural, social, and religious expectations of the Amish community; internally, there was much I rejected. There was a kind of two-way marginalization that kept me from being completely at home in either of the two worlds. I felt secure inside the borders of the Amish world, but it was paradoxical. Being inside the defined borders of my family and the Amish community was a wonderfully secure place to be. I knew where the lines were, and I knew that if I stayed inside those lines, I was safely in. On one side of my brain, so to speak, I knew that I belonged. On the other side, it was not so clear.

Like most families, we had our store of family stories. It was on an afternoon in late fall, after my parents had bought the new place near Stuarts Draft and we had moved, that Mom and 12-year-old Leo were on their way back to the old house to pick up some leftover things, driving our recently purchased horse and buggy along Route

12. Suddenly and without warning, as they recounted it, the horse stopped in his tracks, gave a few shudders, and fell over dead![9]

As it happened a local businessman, Jason, who was known to the Amish (he had actually been instrumental in helping the earliest get established in Stuarts Draft) came along just then. He pulled over and asked, in Pennsylvania Dutch, "Was iss letz?" (What's wrong?) It was a rhetorical question, of course: there was a dead horse lying on the highway with a buggy still attached—and a young Amish woman and her 12-year-old son who needed help. Others had also, by this time, stopped to help, and the dead horse was unhitched, dragged, and rolled off the highway, and the buggy was pulled to the side of the road. Jason then drove Mom and Leo home, where they could get help from Dad, who made arrangements to dispose of the horse and have the empty buggy towed home. Mom said later that she thought Jason, who came by at just the right time, must have been an angel. We came to know Jason and his family as members of the local community—Dad later worked in one of his businesses for a time. I remember him as rather short, balding and decidedly stout. "Angels" can apparently come in all shapes and sizes.

Another often-recited family story begins with a family outing to the mountains along the St. Mary's River and ends with the bear that wasn't killed. The St. Mary's flowed through untamed but scenic mountain country. With rocks in the streambed and waterfalls interspersed with calmer pools, St. Mary's was a popular spot for trout fishing, picnicking, and picking wild blueberries. It was an outing our family made now and again during our growing-up years. Mom was especially fond of the natural world and loved these occasions with her family. We made these excursions with a wagon pulled by our farm tractor—usually with Leo at the wheel and the rest of us piled onto the wagon—something like an extended hayride.

On this occasion, we were on our way home in the late afternoon, tired but in good spirits. Leo was, as usual, driving the tractor with the rest of us on the wagon. The road leading out of the mountains was one of those narrow but scenic, curving, single-track backroads common in rural Virginia at the time. Farm tractors don't travel very fast, so there was plenty of time to smell the roadside grasses and enjoy the dappled shadows from the trees overhead.

I remember our surprise when, rounding a bend, there was a woman standing in the road waving both arms wildly. She was shouting something about chickens and a bear. "Help! There's a bear in my chicken house! You need to shoot it! It's killing my chickens!" We stopped, of course, but Dad and Leo were uncertain about whether they were up to facing a hungry bear in a chicken coop. For one thing, of course, they didn't have a gun and said so. "I have a gun," she yelled, "It's a bear gun...use it... quick!" Still uncertain about facing a bear, even with a bear gun, they followed her around the house and out of our sight. The rest of us waited expectantly for the sound of the bear gun. But there was no sound. After what seemed like a long time Leo and Dad reappeared, looking distinctly relieved. The bear had left before they got there. Leo got back onto the trac-tor seat and we drove on. I was disappointed, but the story about the bear that wasn't shot was one of the staples in our cache of family tales.

Neither of my parents were educated beyond what they were able to get in their rural, one-room elementary schools in Kansas and Ok-lahoma,[10] but they were, to an extent, self-educated and brought a variety of reading material into our home. In addition to the Bible, they read farming, gardening and nature magazines. They also read periodicals from both the Amish[11] and the more liberal (by Amish standards) Mennonite press—the latter being something of an anom-aly in our Amish community. Now and again, they subscribed to the local newspapers, but would cancel the subscriptions after a few weeks, saying that it wasn't worth the money. Clearly, the newspaper stories were about "them" (the affairs of the non-Amish) and were not very relevant to "us" (the Amish). But reading was, in any case, reserved for spare time. Work came first. If one of us children "had our nose in a book" when there was work to be done, they would be told to put the book down and get to work. It was a refrain I learned from memory while growing up.

Unlike many other Amish communities, the Amish in Stuarts Draft did not have their own school for the community's first couple of decades, but sent their children to the local public schools. For the Amish families living in Stuarts Draft, sending their children to the public school, may have been influenced by the knowledge that the principal was an elder in a local church and the senior 7th grade teacher was a Mennonite minister—both of whom were known and trusted by the Amish. So, like my Amish cohorts in Stuarts Draft, I attended the public elementary school[12] through 7th grade. It was a quite large school for being in a rural area with something over 600 students at that time—a major change for the westerners whose school experiences had been limited to the one-room schools of rural Kansas and Oklahoma. The catchment area of the Stuarts Draft public school was large and included children from the surrounding foothills and mountains as well as the hamlets and farms scattered across our county. There were no children of color at our school.

Elementary school was, for me, a generally happy and positive time. Though I only became fluent in English after beginning school (Pennsylvania Dutch was the common language of the Amish, and usually spoken in most Amish homes), I could understand and speak it well enough to get along (being surrounded by "English" neighbors was definitely a factor). But I learned quickly and soon became a voracious reader, spending hours (too many, my mother said) reading whatever I could lay my hands on. There were only a few other Amish children in my grade (to my disappointment, they were all girls), but we were, for the most part, accepted by our fellow classmates. The teachers were quick to squelch any mocking or making fun of the Amish kids and went out of their way to demonstrate acceptance and understanding of the Amish children's differentness.

I did well academically and gained a reputation among my teachers and classmates as a bookworm. But I was klutzy in sports and dreaded the humiliation of always being one of the last ones to be chosen for softball or dodgeball. (It didn't help much when, in an obvious effort to be nice, someone would reverse the order and pick us klutzes first. Everyone still knew we were the klutzes.)

I tended to be shy but responded to teachers or classmates who made overtures and I made a few close school friends. Though we were good friends at school, we rarely visited each other's homes or played with each other outside of school. I was especially pleased when, in the 7th grade, my best friend, Billy, and I were selected to be the "ice cream sellers" in the school cafeteria. Billy's family lived in the foothills and our home cultures were probably as different as could be, but we found common ground and hung out together a lot during our free time. Both of us were pleased when the principal once called us brothers.

I suspect that my positive experience among the "English" in elementary school may have played a role in helping me feel comfortable among "outsiders" in later life though it seemed clear to me at the time that I could never belong to that world. School also gave me the confidence that I could succeed by the standards of the English world. But it also strengthened the keen awareness of how different I was from them—I had to wear funny clothes and had an Amish haircut. They all had cars and watched movies; my parents wouldn't[t even know how to drive a car, I thought, much less own one.[13] And they certainly believed watching movies was wrong!

By the time I was in the upper elementary grades, the county school board had begun to enforce an attendance law that children must stay in school until their 16th birthday. Up until that time, it had been acceptable in our county for children to drop out after completing the 7th grade. The new law (or at least its enforcement) meant that the Amish would have to keep their children in school for 2-3 years beyond 7th grade. Since sending them to the public high school was out of the question, they chose, with approval by the County School Board, to build their own one-room high school where the Amish children could attend until they reached the legal age for quitting.

This was the school to which I was sent after completing 7th grade. Teachers (there was only one at a time; it was a one-room school) did not have to be qualified and typically had not formally completed high school themselves. They taught from the book, barely staying ahead of their students in the often-out-of-date texts donated by the local school district. Like my Amish peers, I dropped out a few weeks before my sixteenth birthday and began working full time with Dad on our farm.

From the perspective of the Amish church leaders and parents, this system served them well; ostensibly providing some basic education that their children might need to be successful farmers and housewives while, at the same time, satisfying the school authorities. But my brief experience in the Amish school had kind of an ironic twist. On the one hand, I was dismissive of the school as I experienced it. Though I never got into serious trouble and got good enough grades with very little effort, I didn't take the schooling very seriously—something that was not missed by the teacher and that was regularly reflected in her comments on my report card. But I actually loved learning outside of school, and read almost everything I could get my hands on. I loved literature and poetry. Sometimes, after I'd quit school, I'd stick a small book of poetry into my pocket when I was doing field work with a tractor, and would read aloud to myself over the noise of the engine. After we had joined a more liberal branch of Amish that permitted cars, and I was old enough to drive, a friend and I would drive several miles to the public library when they had evening hours. We browsed the shelves and checked out a few books each time. The Amish church leaders would not have been pleased had they known, but the library was still another window into worlds outside of my closed Amish one.

The popular press, cheap fiction, Amish romance novels and entertainment media have sensationalized and cheapened the image of the Amish people and their culture. But those depictions are a far cry from the Amish world and the Amish people as I experienced them. Though I would leave the community, church, and culture, my experience of growing up in a strong Amish family that was, itself, deeply embedded within a tightly knit Amish church and culture felt safe and secure. I still respect the integrity of that community. They were, for the most part, sincere people who believed deeply in their church, in its traditions and practices. As I would come to realize much later, the legacy of that community still forms part of who I am and how I see and understand myself in the world.

Church was an integral part of our family life. It was the social and cultural center, as well as the religious center, of our Amish community. There was never any question or discussion about whether one would attend church on a Sunday morning or whether one could miss any of the other church community activities. Life revolved around the church and its activities.

The Amish in Stuarts Draft were "Church Amish," meaning that while indisputably Amish, they were by comparison, a bit more progressive, allowing electricity in their houses and farms and allowing tractors with rubber tires.[15] Not only did they farm with these tractors, they also used them for local travel during the week, though not on Sunday. Though it was looked at a bit askance by some of the more conservative ministers, some even installed special overdrive gears in their tractors to make them go faster. But the horse and buggy must be used to go to church or church meetings. Because there is no central conference or organizational structure among the Amish, local congregations have power to decide on their own rules and practice, though churches with similar rules often form a loose association and would, for example, invite ministers from their sister congregations to preach in one of their services. Congregations that deviated too far from the norm of a given group would, on the other hand, be considered "out of fellowship" with their group of churches.

The interior of our church building was plain; the woodwork and homemade, straight-backed, wooden pews all of unpainted wood. Behind the church building there was a long, low stable for the horses. Though allowed in the homes, there was no electricity and running water in the church building. Entry to the building was through one of two vestibules—one at each end of the building. The one in the front[16] was for women and girls and the one in the back, closer to the horse barn, for the men and boys. Each vestibule had rows of hooks on the walls where the women and girls, in their end, could hang their bonnets and shawls[17] and where the men and boys, in the opposite vestibule, could hang their (always black) hats—and overcoats in cold weather. The women and girls were dropped off at their entrance as each buggy arrived; the men then drove the horse and buggy further into the church yard where they would unhitch the horse and lead it into the stable.

The women and the men, either of whom might have small children in tow, would enter the church from their respective ends of the building, greeting each other, then making their way to their places: men on one side and women on the other. The young unmarried men, the adolescent boys, and the little (elementary age) boys would gather outside or, when it was cold, in the anteroom at the end of the building, their female counterparts doing the same on the other end. As if on a signal, just as it was time for the service to begin (somebody would actually check a watch[18]) the young men and boys and the young women and girls would file into the building in long rows from opposite ends of the building to their pre-assigned places. The older (unmarried, roughly age 16 and above) young people filing into their places first, followed by the adolescents, which were in turn followed by the elementary-aged children; each into their respective, gender-divided sections.

The ministers preached without notes, though some seemed to have prepared their remarks in advance, while others seemed to depend on the inspiration of the moment. As in Kansas, services were conducted in a mixture of Pennsylvania Dutch, (the everyday language of the Amish), and Martin Luther's 16th century high German which was used for the hymns and Bible reading. For small children, the earliest years of Sunday School were when they learned to read the German Bible. Services were typically about 3 hours long, beginning and ending with several songs, led from the pews by one or more informally acknowledged "fore-singers" from among the men. (Women did not lead singing nor did they speak in church.) There were typically two sermons; the first, the "anfang" (the opening or beginning) was usually somewhat shorter and more or less devotional in nature. This would be followed by a longer, main sermon which typically consisted of exhortation to right living and obedience to God (as interpreted by the Amish from the German scriptures) and to the church "ordnung" (rules). On most Sundays the main speaker, after finishing, would ask one or more men from the congregation to give testimony to what they had heard. This was the church setting in which I formed my earliest, implicit understandings of church and what it meant.

When I was 13 years old, the Amish church in Stuarts Draft split, members disagreeing on issues they each considered important. The more progressive wing, though still considering themselves to be Amish and retaining many of the Amish norms and traditions, wanted to allow cars and telephones while the more conservative resisted. My family, without much discussion in the hearing of us children—though I'm sure there was discussion that we didn't hear, especially with fellow Kansans Uncle Ben and Aunt Mary—joined with the more liberal movement, known as "Beachy[19] Amish." Following the split, the Beachy group in Stuarts Draft built a new church building a few miles away on land donated by one of the group's ministers. Members of the new group began buying and driving cars and trucks (which had to be black and could not sport too much chrome) and installing telephones in their houses—my parents among them. Their new church building, though still plain and simple, was electrified and had running water. The services, however, were still mostly in the traditional mixture of Pennsylvania Dutch and German. In hindsight, it was not always clear why families chose to join or not join the Beachy group, certainly there were different reasons for different people. Being allowed to buy and drive cars was no doubt reason enough for some. Others were likely reacting to what they perceived as an overly strict adherence to the "ordnung" (rules) of the original group. Significantly, few members of the original group that had founded the Stuarts Draft community chose to affiliate with the Beachy group. For them, the split no doubt felt like *deja vu*, reliving the divisions in the Tidewater area some years ago.

Many of the customs from the old church, including most of the regulations about dress and the use of Pennsylvania Dutch and Luther's German, continued. Though there was some effort to reach out to the surrounding communities, these practices would have been major roadblocks should any non-Amish have considered joining their church (which, to my knowledge, never happened). I was baptized into this church in my mid-teens. Though I was more or less following the expectations for young people my age, it was something I took seriously, despite lingering questions about Amish belief and practice that were never satisfactorily answered.

While the Amish church, as I experienced it, would have understood itself to be a Christian denomination (though clearly different than other denominations), being Amish was also much more than that. The traditions and beliefs within which I grew up were expressions of a strong cultural and social context with clearly defined boundaries, some of which were formal and explicit—the church ordnung for example—while others were just understood. The more explicit "ordnung" (most of which, to my knowledge, was unwritten), if violated, would trigger a formal rebuke or sanction by the bishop or the congregation. Other practices were just the accepted norm—"the way we do things"—such as gender roles in the home and church, for example, or of how children should behave (generally "seen but not heard." Young children were trained at an early age to sit quietly during long services.) While not having the weight of "ordnung," such expectations were still clearly understood and were, for the most part, followed. Sanctions in such cases were also informal—becoming the subject of community gossip for example—but deviation from even these informal rules was relatively rare. Obedience to parents and conforming to expectations were high virtues of the Amish community.

Church conflicts often developed into a kind of passive resistance, which sometimes escalated into open confrontation. Conflict, if not resolved, often led to distancing: a mode of conflict resolution that was, to one degree or another, responsible for the numerous church divisions among the Amish that not infrequently led to one faction moving to another location and beginning a new church. I was a generally compliant young person whose instinct was to avoid conflict, nor did I like calling attention to myself, so I mostly colored inside the lines, though I often argued against them internally, where I would question the basis for church authority. Sometimes I found ways to walk just as close to the lines as I could without calling attention to myself or triggering a reprimand.[20]

The youth group in the Stuarts Draft Beachy Amish church organized activities such as hymn singings or social events. The youth group was, ostensibly, under the oversight of an adult, though the adult didn't usually show up or interfere, so long as the youth engaged in approved activities such as singing for the elderly at nursing homes or preparing boxes of food for the needy at Thanksgiving. The youth annually elected a group leader who would give overall leadership to the group. He (The elected leader was always a male; female influence was indirect and behind the scenes) would serve as spokesperson for the group and was more or less responsible for ensuring that activities were scheduled and managed appropriately within the boundaries.

In due course, I was elected group leader. My parents had allowed me to join the youth group while I was a year or so younger than most (no doubt triggering some comments by other parents), and so I was probably among the youngest members of the group to have been elected. However, I was affirmed by others and served, I believe, a couple of terms. Shy though I was, I found leadership to somehow feel natural and gained unexpected satisfaction and energy in the role, though to have said so publicly would have been unacceptable and a violation of the important Amish virtue of *demut*[21] (humility).

I was about 9 or 10 when Dad was offered the opportunity to rent a nearby dairy farm. We could buy the cows and the farm equipment on good terms and farm the land. In return, the owner would get a percentage of the monthly milk check. Dad had been working at various jobs, such as carpentry or in a chick hatchery, since moving to Virginia, none of which paid especially well or were very satisfying. This offer held the possibility of returning to his roots as a farmer and to being his own boss once again, but without taking on a large debt. After consulting with Mom and getting advice from others, he accepted the offer.

Renting the farm (something his own father had done years before in western Oklahoma) turned out to be a good move; the financial terms were fair, and the farm became a family project with different members of the family playing different roles at different times, depending on their age and availability. During the early years—until he left home around age 21—Leo played a major role, with my sisters helping out as needed. Though I sometimes rebelled against the work—especially getting up at 5:00 every morning to do the milking—and though I rebelled against even the notion of ever becoming a farmer myself—the farm was to have an outsize impact on my growing up years. I learned what it meant to be entrusted with major responsibilities, gaining confidence in my ability to make decisions and carry them out. I also discovered a deep-seated love of nature and of being in the outdoors. This was the setting in which I lived and worked until I left home, just before turning 21.

The farm was also the setting for drama on occasion. There was, for example a midnight fire,[22] when I was 9 or 10, that destroyed a large, two story chicken house with thousands of young chicks inside. The intense heat from the chicken house fire melted the metal roof on the nearby dairy barn and set the hay ablaze. Fortunately, all of the livestock (except the baby chicks) were saved. I was too young to be anything but an observer, but saving the cows and moving most of the farm equipment to safety was, without doubt, a coming-of-age experience for 18-year-old Leo. As is typical of the Amish (and the non-Amish as well) the community came together afterward to offer support and, in the Amish tradition, took the lead in cleaning up the mess; then organizing a barn raising to rebuild the barn roof in record time

Then there was the incident with the skittish cow. It happened on a warm evening in late summer; I was left with a broken right leg and a reinforced love of reading, not to mention an antipathy for cows in general. I was 11 years old. Our dairy operation used vacuum-powered milking machines that hung by a strap over the cow's back while she was being milked. We used 2 or 3 of the machines at a time, and as each cow was finished, the milk would be dumped into a collection pail, and the machine would leapfrog to the next cow. The strap had a long, curved metal rod attached to one end that would pass under the cow's belly and be hooked into an eyelet on the opposite end of the strap. To hang the strap, one first passed the end with the metal rod over the cow's back, then reached under her to grasp the rod, brought it under the cow's belly, and hooked it into the eyelet. There were always a few more straps than milking machines, so that a strap could be put in place on the next cow ahead of the milking machine...a good job for a kid who wasn't yet strong enough to do much else.

On this evening, I was hanging the straps as I'd done many times before. But this time, one of the cows who was known to be a bit skittish was apparently surprised while in one of her favorite daydreams. Just as I was bending under her belly to pick up the metal rod, she kicked forward with her right rear leg, hitting me in the face and knocking me over. The next thing I remember was lying in the gutter behind Bertie with a strange feeling in my right leg, sort of like it was detached from the rest of me. As the story was reconstructed later, after being knocked down, I had apparently rolled toward Bertie's rear legs while she, excited by the commotion, began dancing about and, in the process, stepped on my right leg above the knee, fracturing the bone in a messy, splintered break.

Dad, of course, had seen what was happening and quickly pulled me out of harm's way, and sent someone to the filling station, about a quarter mile down the road, to ask for someone to take me to the hospital. I still remember who showed up: one of our neighbors known as Shorty. Shorty was a truck driver and had just bought a new "two-tone" black and white 1954 Buick. It was a "hard top convertible" (meaning it had no side posts between the door frame and the roof) which proved to be important because the improvised stretcher—an old ironing board—on which I had been put by then, could more easily be lifted through the side window onto the back seat where it rested on the armrests on the ends of the seat.

I don't recall much about the trip to the small hospital in Waynesboro, about 8 miles away, but vividly remember my pain as well as the beads of sweat that began showing on the surgeon's forehead as he struggled to set the break. The jagged ends of the broken bone were apparently snagged on each other and kept them from slipping into place. After some time, the surgeon gave up and ordered a contraption to be rigged over my hospital bed with weights on one end of a rope that was fastened, on the other end, to my right foot—the idea being that the constant pull of the weights might gradually pull the bones into place.

It didn't work. After two weeks in the hospital bed with the weights attached—and me with considerable pain—the break was still not set. There was some talk about possibly doing surgery to set the break, but after considering the alternatives, my parents decided against it. So, it was decided to let nature heal the bones as they were. I would now go through life with a misaligned bone in my right leg, leaving it slightly longer than the left one. I was wrapped in a plaster body-cast extending from just under my rib-cage to the toes of my right leg and discharged from the hospital. I lived in the cast for the next two weeks or so. I could be propped up to a sort of half-sitting position in bed, but had to be carried from place to place. The cast was removed after two weeks, but I was not allowed to walk for another two weeks. Then, still not allowed to put weight on the healing leg, I graduated to crutches, which I used for another couple of weeks. By the time it was all over, having been off my feet or on crutches for weeks, I had to learn to balance and walk all over again.

I made a couple of special, non-Amish friends while in the hospital. One was Richard, an older gentleman with whom I shared the hospital room for several days. He worked in a furniture factory, and after we had both been discharged, he made a beautiful small table of mahogany and brought it to me at our house. The other was a Black man, James, a hospital attendant who took a special interest in me, and we developed a friendship. He was always cheerful and did his best to cheer me up when I was discouraged and homesick. He seemed to genuinely care about me and had a wonderful personal touch. After I left the hospital, he drove out to our house once to see me. Unfortunately, I didn't stay in touch with either of these men, but their friendship, beyond the pleasure of the friendship itself, offered yet another brief glimpse through a window into a world that to this 11-year-old Amish boy seemed both foreign and fascinating. James spoke of his two young daughters and of doing things together. I met his daughters once when they came to the hospital with James. They must have been maybe 6 and 8, but I remember their shy smiles, though they were too bashful to say much. I had known that Black families existed, of course, but this was the first time I'd come to know a Black man and members of his family as real people.

Keeping an active eleven-year-old occupied and happy over eight weeks of convalescence was, I'm sure, challenging for my family. My sisters were shanghaied into playing games with me, and Mom sometimes arranged playdates with friends, but my mainstay was books. School was not in session when the accident happened, but Mom arranged with the local branch of the public library for a stack of books to be delivered every week. When school started a bit later, the 5th-grade teacher, in whose class I would be when I returned to school, brought books from school as well as some assignments that I could do at home. I was already a voracious reader, but now books had become a lifeline. (My reading tastes were omnivorous: though I especially liked books about nature, science.)

As I grew older, I was given increasing responsibility for the day-to-day work on the farm and was trusted to do much of it without direct supervision. After I left school at age 16, the farm became my full-time job, and I was, in many ways, treated as a young adult. But it wasn't until much later that I realized the remarkable degree of both freedom and responsibility my parents had given me at a young age. On several occasions my parents were away for a few weeks at a time attending a funeral or visiting relatives and left me, a lad of maybe 17 or 18 in charge of the dairy operation—with important assistance from whichever of my sisters might be home at the time. Leo, by that time, was married and in medical training.

I was about that age when Dad joined a small group of farmers who formed a crew each fall to help each other with "silo filling:"—using a tractor-drawn chopper to harvest corn in the field and blow it into a silo for winter feed. The operation required several tractors, wagons and machinery, and a crew of men to operate them. The crew would rotate from one farm to the next until all the corn was cut and blown into the silos. Because we owned the cutter and had a tractor powerful enough to operate it, the job of operating the tractor and chopper fell to me. Running the chopper was a man's job and central to the entire operation. The person operating the tractor and chopper needed to have the skill and judgement to operate complex machinery and keep the entire operation moving. Being accepted as an equal and with a key role to play among the adult men of the crew was tremendously empowering; discovering that I could be a "man among men" was a coming-of-age experience for me.

My years of growing up on the farm also engendered a love of nature and the out-of-doors—caught perhaps, from my mother who loved birds and flowers. (My interest, as an adult, in bird watching and nature photography[23] was no doubt nourished by these boyhood experiences.) Years later, I came to realize this sense of place as offering a kind of rootedness and belonging to the land that played an important role in my coming to understand myself. A few of the places on our farm are etched in memory. There was, for example, the hill on the far end of the back pasture, known (for unknown reasons) as White Hill. There were limestone boulders and, growing between them, huge oaks and black walnut trees. From the summit, we could see for miles, and every fall, Mom would organize a family expedition to gather walnuts, which would later be hulled and cracked. I loved to wander there—usually accompanied by a dog—and sit on a grassy spot under the oaks and look out over the valley below.

A short distance south of the tracks that crossed Stuarts Draft's Main Street, there was a sharp bend in the creek (the South River) that created a natural swimming hole. Often, at the end of a hot summer day of farm work, my friend Elmer would pick me up in his dad's old Chevrolet pickup, and we'd drive the couple of miles to the swimming hole, where we'd join a half-dozen other teenage Amish lads splashing and diving in the water hole. A rope had been tied to a tree branch above the deep part of the pool, and we loved swinging out on the rope and dropping into the water. The creek, flowing out of the mountains, was always deliciously cold, even during the heat of summer. (Needless to say, there were no girls present.) But an hour or so in the creek's cold water left us feeling totally refreshed. Some of the Amish families in the community looked a bit askance at this and wouldn't let their sons take part, though I never understood why. In hindsight, it seems that most of the swimming hole gang eventually left the Amish community in Stuarts Draft for various reasons and in various ways. Maybe swimming near the margins of church approved practice, though seemingly innocuous, was one of the ways the stage was set for the separations that came later.

Another of the memorable places was actually on a neighbor's farm, though I only went there once. We referred to it as the Fitzgerald place; it lay catty-cornered across the highway from our house. Behind their farm buildings was a pasture backed by a patch of woodland. We passed their farm several times a day and, like many over-familiar things, never paid it much attention. But early one spring morning, when there were no immediate chores that had to be done, I decided on a whim to wander through the Fitzgerald woodlot. I often wandered through the woods and fields of our farm, typically with my dog Mike and one or more volumes of Zim's Golden Nature Guides in my pocket. But I had never been to the Fitzgerald woods. I wasn't even quite sure if I might be trespassing since I hadn't asked for permission.

The Fitzgerald woodlot was unremarkable—just another wooded lot, like many in our part of the Shenandoah Valley. Their cattle were pastured there and free to roam the woods at will; the ridged cow paths roughly mapped the contours of the hillside below the woods. I climbed the roadside fence that day, wandered into the woods, and it was there that I found it. Pushing through a thicket of pine saplings, I emerged into a small grass-covered clearing. In the center of the clearing was an oval-shaped pool of bright, clear water, reflecting the sky and clouds like a mirror. Framing the pool was the most brilliantly green carpet of soft grass I'd ever seen and, behind it, the thicket of young pine saplings standing guard in a still different shade of green. The clearing was hidden; maybe I was the only human to ever see it: a reflecting pool holding the sky and clouds inside a frame of soft grass, all held in the embrace of the young pines that encircled it.

It was a vernal pool; it would likely dry up in the summer. But for me, at that moment, it was magic. Maybe it was the sheer surprise of finding it there, but I remember sitting down at the pool's edge, mesmerized. Mike came over and leaned against me. Maybe he too felt a little of the magic. For the next minutes—I have no idea how long—there was only me and Mike and an enchanted clearing in the woods. I can relive the impression as though it were yesterday. I never told anyone about it; they wouldn't have understood. It was a secret that only Mike and I knew about.

Another favorite was some four miles up the road from the main farm—a kind of satellite farm. We called it the Stump Place—after a previous owner. There was a creek running through it, and we pastured cattle on the hills beyond. We grew corn and alfalfa in the open fields on the near side.

To get there, one turned from the highway onto a rough lane that ran through woods. There were potholes in the lane that became mud holes after a rain. A half-mile or so from the turn-off, the lane emerged into open fields with overgrown fence rows dividing the fields from each other. The creek and pasture could be seen further on. Separated from the highway and with no human habitation visible in any direction, one had the sense of being completely alone with the woods, the overgrown fence rows, and the pasture beyond. Muskrats, raccoons, and the occasional mink made their homes along the creek, and foxes, deer, and, very rarely, a black bear came down from the nearby foothills to hunt or graze or to just pass through.

Just beyond the pasture gate, a small cluster of dilapidated sheds marked the one-time farmyard. A short distance further, on a low bluff overlooking the creek, was a long-deserted, antebellum plantation house. It stood above a fresh-water spring that rippled over stones and ran through beds of watercress and spearmint on its way to the creek. Many of the windows had long been broken out, and the few remaining shutters dangled haphazardly. The doors stood half-opened, and small animals were obviously coming and going at will. But the house still carried, somehow, proud reminders of its former grandeur and its once-upon-a-time elegance, now forlorn and for-saken. On the walls of the main rooms, there were still traces of sten-ciled grapevines with what appeared to be roses growing improbably among them. It was easy to imagine well-dressed ladies and gentle-men coming down the broad central staircase into the hall. What would have been the kitchen and servants' quarters were off to the side. There was a kind of fascinating melancholy about the place, a palpable sense of a once-grand world now gone.

I spent many hours at the Stump Place, sometimes working, sometimes just fooling around along the creek, looking for muskrat tracks or picking mulberries from the gigantic mulberry tree near the house. Sometimes I needed to search the pasture for a newborn calf whose mother had done her best to hide it. Once, some pals and I built a raft that we floated in one of the deeper pools of the creek. (It didn't work very well. The raft kept tipping, dumping its pas-sengers into the creek.) There was a quietness and peace about the place—only the noises, sights and smells of nature and scant evidence of humans in any direction. The image still has the power, even to-day, to evoke a kind of wistful nostalgia; long ago memories of a time and place that now seem innocent and carefree.

++++++

[1] The actual relationship was complicated. By the time Uncle Ed moved to Stuarts Draft, he had married for the third time. His first wife was a daughter of Eli Nisly, thus a sister to Mary and my mother. His second wife was a half-sister to Uncle Ben and my

grandfather John D. and thus a "half-aunt" to my father. The third wife was unrelated to our family.

[2] This is a rough and rounded number that is roughly pegged to the beginnings of the Amish church in Switzerland in the late 17th century.

[3] A small but typical example: the Western Amish permitted fold-over collars and pockets on men's (and boys') shirts while the "Eastern rules" did not allow them. If a ready-made men's or boy's shirt was purchased at a store (frowned upon in the early days but later a common practice), the fold-over part of the collar and the pocket had to be removed.

[4] So-called tenant houses were a common feature of farms in that part of Virginia. The farm owner would live in the large "main house" while a farm worker's family would occupy the "tenant house," which would then be considered part of his compensation. The tenant houses were almost always smaller and located in a less prominent part of the farm. If there were no farm worker families available to live in the tenant house, it might be rented out.

[5] Since then, several large manufacturing firms and warehouses have moved into the area and the economy is now a mix of manufacturing and agriculture.

[6] There are other stories that claim to account for the name. An alternate version references an old English usage where a "draft" was something extracted from something larger. Thomas Stuart's land was extracted from his father's larger tract, hence: "Stuarts Draft."

[7] The first Amish actually moved to Stuarts Draft from the Virginia Beach area in 1942.

[8] Threshing crews were a common feature of farms before wide use of "combines." Farmers in a community would agree to share labor for harvesting and threshing grain, moving from one farm to the next as the grain ripened. Extra labor was sometimes hired as needed. "Dinner" (the mid-day meal) would be provided by the farm whose

crop was being harvested that day. Typically, all of the threshing crew would be served at a large common table.

[9] It was later determined that the horse had been suffering from "heaves," a disorder something like COPD in humans, and that an honest horse trader would never have sold it to an unsuspecting buyer. It wasn't long before the dead horse was replaced by a long-legged, gray mare named Queen. Queen was famous for shedding her gray/white hair that floated out behind her and stuck to the clothes of whoever was sitting in the buggy. We, like all Amish, wore dark or black clothes to church, so we always had to brush white horse hair from our Sunday clothes after arriving at church.

[10]My mother said she repeated 5th grade three times. Not because she failed the work (In fact she appears to have done well), but because her father (my grandfather who was also the bishop of their church) believed that education beyond fifth grade was superfluous and unnecessary. A fifth-grade education was all that was needed to read the Bible and get along in the world. My father, growing up in a different community and thus under a different bishop, completed 7th grade.

[11] To my knowledge, there was at that time only one Amish periodical, published monthly and in German: *Herald der Wahrheit* (Herold of Truth), and a weekly newspaper, catering to Amish and conservative Mennonites: *The Budget*. The Mennonite press published several weekly and monthly magazines, a couple of which were specifically aimed at children and youth.

[12] Even though the Amish church in which I grew up no longer exists, their (somewhat more liberal) daughter congregation in Stuarts Draft now has their own K-12 school.

[13] That changed, of course, when my parents sided with the more liberal Amish group that allowed cars.

[14] Amish churches and communities across the country, while sharing many basic beliefs and practices, nevertheless vary consider-

ably from one location to the next. I write about the Amish as I experienced them.

[15] I don't know why the more conservative Amish churches drew this line. Perhaps it was an arbitrary line intended to avoid modernity. Perhaps it was to guard against what did in fact happen: that tractors with rubber tires would make it too easy for them to be used like automobiles.

[16] The building was actually situated "sideways" so that none of the entrance doors faced the road.

[17] Women and girls were not allowed to wear coats or sweaters that had sleeves to church, though they could be worn for "everyday work" on the farm. Men and boys, on the other hand, wore (handmade) coats or jackets. Young men would begin wearing a "Sunday suit coat" after they had been baptized and joined the church. It would be a short frock coat, called a "mutza," without lapels or pockets similar to the "Nehru jacket" of the 1970s, but with a vent in the back and closed with hooks and eyes instead of buttons. In warm weather, they might wear only a vest that was also part of the same suit.

[18] It would be a pocket watch, of course. Wrist watches were not allowed.

[19] The Beachy Amish were named after the group's founder, who had led a movement in Western Pennsylvania in the late 1920s to break away from the Old Order Amish church.

[20] It was easy, for example, when safely away from the likelihood of being spotted by anyone from the Amish community, to comb my hair differently (Amish rules required hair to be parted in the middle) or wear a jacket or coat in such a way that it wasn't easy to see that I was wearing "Amish clothes" underneath.

[21] To be prideful was a kind of "cardinal sin" in the Amish (largely unwritten) lexicon.

[22] This happened soon after we began renting the farm. One of the heaters for the chicks apparently malfunctioned and overheated,

setting fire to the wooden building with tar paper siding. Once ig-
nited, there was no stopping it in spite of the best efforts of three fire
companies.

[23] The Amish didn't allow cameras of course, so I didn't own a
camera until I had left home.

{ **four** }

Oklahoma

For a deep understanding of my family narrative—the narrative by which I try to understand myself—one needs to explore the upstream headwaters. Of course, the choice of how far upstream one goes to begin the exploration is arbitrary. Though I never lived in Oklahoma, my family narrative was shaped by those who did. My mother's family at first lived in Kansas, and my father's family in Western Oklahoma. The two families came together when they both moved to Nowata County in Eastern Oklahoma.

The Depression years of the 1930s and early 1940s were accompanied and followed by the Dust Bowl, when large swaths of Oklahoma, Texas, and Southwestern Kansas suffered through years of drought and crop failure. The winds that blew across the plains sucked up not only what little moisture might have been in the soil, but picked up the bone-dry soil itself, forming huge dust clouds that carried topsoil from one county or from one state to the next. Dust settled, so we were told, like orange-brown snow drifts around anything in its path. Farm families probably suffered the most, receiving scant relief from either nature or from their government. Some despaired, packed the remnants of their belongings, and followed the rumors of better opportunities in California.

But the Amish communities of my parents chose to stay—they really had few other options. They were dirt-poor, living in a tough world where only the most resourceful survived. Money was scarce, and they learned to make do with what they had. The children, we

were told—and some of the adults too, for that matter—went bare-
foot whenever the weather allowed, thus saving their one pair of
shoes for the coldest weather and for those rare occasions when they
needed to dress up. If they were lucky, there would still be enough
wear left in the shoes after they'd been outgrown to pass them down
to the next child in line. The close-knit Amish communities—many
of whose members were also blood relatives—learned to be self-re-
liant, while at the same time depending on each other when they
needed support and help. Community members stood ready to help
each other with field work and shared tools and farm equipment. The
women helped each other harvest and preserve vegetables from their
gardens and cared for each other's children when needed. They sat
with each other when there was sickness or a death. The Amish communities stood (or fell) together. This was the world of my parents
and, indirectly, the one into which I was born.

It was in the late 1920s that my maternal grandfather, Amish
Bishop Eli Nisly, made a decision that would change his life and the
lives of his descendants. Central Kansas, where he had been married
and where he was raising his family, did not, he came to believe, hold
a viable future for his children and their families.

Eli Nisly had come to Kansas with his siblings and his recently
widowed father from an Amish community in Illinois at age 19. His
father died two years after the move, leaving the family orphaned.
Soon afterward, Eli traveled to relatives in Indiana, asking their help
to find someone willing to come to Kansas to keep house for their
now parentless family. A young Amish-Mennonite[1] woman, Fannie
Troyer[2], whose own mother had passed away some years earlier, and
who had been working as a maid while still a very young girl, was
recommended. Eli approached her, and she agreed to accompany him
as a housekeeper. The match was apparently a good one as, some two
years later, she and Eli were married—a marriage that was to last
more than 50 years. Fannie was 19 and Eli was 23 at the time. They
would go on to have a family of thirteen children.

As time passed and land prices in central Kansas climbed, Eli worried about his children's future and whether he could help his sons and sons-in-law establish themselves and their families on farms of their own, as was the expectation among the Amish. After several exploratory trips in Kansas and adjoining states, Eli settled on Nowata County, in the northeast corner of Oklahoma, where farmland sold for as low as $29 an acre (compared to more than $100 an acre in central Kansas). Nowata County seemed a promising location for forming a new Amish community. Eli believed that his children and their families, along with other unrelated Amish families who might join them, could settle there and, given the relatively low land prices, begin to thrive. He envisioned a community where his children and grandchildren could put down roots and where they might find like-minded mates from among the Amish in their own community.

Though tribal lands surrounded them, there seemed to be little recognition by the Amish (nor, I suspect, of most of the non-Amish) that the land they lived on had first been home to indigenous peoples. These peoples had been forcibly displaced when the state of Oklahoma gave their land away in a series of so-called Land Rushes. At an earlier time, Nowata had been declared by the town's boosters to have "the world's shallowest oil deposits." These oil fields led to several boom years for Nowata during the early 1900s, but the boom clearly faded as the century progressed.

One of my mother's older sisters, Mary, who was married and had a young family, was among the first of the Nisly clan to move to Nowata in 1931. My mother, unmarried then, went along to help care for the children. But Eli, the founding patriarch, didn't actually move there until 1934. As bishop of congregations in Kansas, he felt an obligation to them and felt that he would be deserting them if he moved away before another leader was in place. So, in the early years of the Nowata community, Eli divided his time between Kansas and Oklahoma. Sometimes he and Fannie traveled by hired car between their home in Kansas and the Nowata community. On a few occasions, they made the 200-mile journey by horse and buggy, stopping for the night with farm families along the way.

Eli had been chosen for the ministry by "lot,"[3] as was—and still is—the custom for choosing ministers and bishops among the Amish. The decision to become a minister (and later a bishop) was not a choice or decision he made, but was something he accepted and embraced as God's call and God's will. Eli was ordained to the ministry in his mid-twenties. Some twenty years later, he was ordained bishop—an overseer of a district of Amish churches—also by "lot." However, the candidates would have been restricted to those already ordained ministers.

Though it seems Eli left few written records of his life or his work, he was, by all accounts, well respected for his relational skills and his abilities as a preacher, though he never flourished economically. Though he had a reputation of being conservative—and was, we were told, very strict with his children—he appears to have been widely welcomed as a visiting preacher and a good problem solver. He and Fannie traveled regularly to the churches under his charge and to congregations in adjoining districts and states.

My father's family, on the other hand, the John D. Yoder family (the 'D' was important[4] to distinguish him from all of the other John Yoders in Amish communities) had been living in Western Oklahoma near the small town of Weatherford. Though like the Nislys, they were Amish farmers, they came to Nowata under different circumstances and from a still more rural and less populated region, where living conditions were rugged and where farming was unpredictable. The farms around Weatherford were widely scattered; some families lived miles from their nearest neighbors or the nearest town. A heavy rain, snow, or a spring thaw could turn the roads into mud and make them nearly impassable, even for a horse and wagon. A trip to town could be an all-day event even under good conditions.

My grandfather, John D, was born in Western Indiana, and he was the firstborn son of his father, Dan, and Dan's first wife,

Lucy. Lucy passed away when John was three, and for the next number of months John was cared for by different relatives until Dan remarried, and small John could once again live with his own family. After a move by the family to a newly founded Amish community in Mississippi, Dan's second wife also passed away. John was 13. Dan married a third time and, when the short-lived Amish community in Mississippi broke up, moved his family to Central Kansas (Reno County, near Hutchinson) where his third wife, John's second stepmother, also passed away a year or two after John had left home.

Three years after the move to Reno County, John D "came of age,"[5] and moved to Oklahoma, where, in the spring of 1907, he married "Katie" (Catherine) Miller. He was 21 and she was 23. As it happened, Katie was a sister to his father's third wife, Elizabeth. Elizabeth died several months[6] after John D and Katie were married. Still, between the time of their marriage and Elizabeth's passing, John D. was married to his stepmother's sister—his "step aunt"!

Custer County, where John D. and Katie were married and began raising their family, was in western Oklahoma, where the dust bowl had been particularly severe, and times had been hard. John D suffered a series of farming set-backs which, whether because of the weather or from poor management[7] or perhaps some of both, had led the bank to foreclose on his farm—first on his livestock, then the farm equipment,[8] and, finally, on the land itself. He had since supported his family by farming on rented land. My father, John D., and Katie's second child and oldest son, turned 21 when his family moved to Nowata in 1932. Dad never talked much about his family's experiences during those hard years in Western Oklahoma—or even much at all about his growing-up years, for that matter. But there's no doubt that those experiences shaped his view of the world and of himself within it—and which became, in turn, part of the "social and cultural DNA" that I and my siblings inherited.

It's not clear why John D. chose to move his family from Custer County to Nowata. County. No doubt there were multiple reasons—economic, for one. It also seems that the Custer County Amish young people had something of a reputation for being undisciplined and it's possible that John D and Katie wanted to bring their children into a different environment. John was 45 years old at the time, and the earlier failure of his farm no doubt weighed on both him and his family. Moving must have seemed an opportunity for a new start. The John D. Yoder family moved to Nowata in January of 1932.

The Yoder and Nisly families would have known each other from the years they were both in Reno County, Kansas, and it would not have escaped John's and Katie's notice that the Nisly family, by then established in Nowata County, had a number of young people approaching marriageable age, as did they. As it turned out, connections between these two families would prove to be remarkably generative. Three Yoder sons would marry Nisly daughters (my parents being the first), John D's half-brother, Ben, had already married into the Nisly family back in Kansas, and another of the Yoder daughters would marry one of Eli and Fannie's grandsons. My parents were married eight months later: the first Amish wedding in that new Amish community. He was 22; she had just turned 27.

As noted above, Ben, a half-brother to John D, had married my mother's next-oldest sister, Mary (making their children something like 1 1/2 cousins to us). My mother and Mary were especially close, and our families spent much time together. The connection between our families was no doubt a factor in my parents' decision to follow Ben and Mary to Eastern Kansas and, still later, to Virginia. In any case, the pairings of the Yoder and Nisly offspring seem to have been extraordinarily fruitful.

By some measures, the Nisly and Yoder families were an unlikely fit: the Yoders had adopted a lifestyle shaped by the hardscrabble economy of dust-bowl Western Oklahoma, where there was little time or energy for niceties. The Nislys, on the other hand, had been living in a more mature, though still rural, economy where they could, to some extent, look beyond day-to-day and year-to-year survival. However, within the broad outlines of Amish belief and culture—not to mention 300 years of shared Swiss ancestry—they understood each other.

The Amish community in Nowata County, Oklahoma, lasted for just about 11 years. After a few years of good rains and good harvests, the elements seemed to turn against the Amish. There was virtually no rain for several years, and when it did come, it could be violent. Even the most stoic farmers could be driven to tears as they watched the crop they were ready to harvest the next day be flattened beyond any semblance of recovery by a sudden hailstorm. Grasshoppers could descend like a cloud without warning and destroy a field of standing corn or a field of wheat within hours. Almost every farmstead had an underground cave or cellar into which the family could take shelter when a tornado was on the horizon. Roads were rudimentary and sometimes impassable; even buggies and horse-drawn wagons could get mired in the sticky, red mud during spring thaw.

The little Amish community's chances of long-term survival were dealt a final blow when its founding leader, Bishop Eli Nisly, died in 1941. Members of the Amish community in Nowata—mostly Yoders and Nislys by this time—came together soon after Eli's death to discuss their options. They decided to sell out and move elsewhere.

By the fall and winter of 1941-1942 all of the Amish who had been living in Nowata County had left; the Yoder-Nisly clan, including widow Fannie Nisly and John D and Katie Yoder, moved to an Amish community in eastern Kansas, near Garnett in Anderson County. By the early months of 1942, all that was left of the Amish community in Nowata County was a small graveyard in the corner of a field that had once been part of Eli Nisly's farm. Simple tombstones marked the burial sites of Bishop Eli Nisly and of several young children who had not survived. Despite the hardship of those years, my parents and other members of the small Amish community living in Nowata

County, Oklahoma, would later reflect on those years as among the best years of their lives.[9]

Many years later, my siblings and I organized a family reunion in Kansas that included a day trip across the border to Nowata. We visited the old cemetery and tried to locate the farms where we believed our parents and relatives had lived. When we stopped by the small public library, an elderly member of the library staff, who was now retired but who happened to be there that day, told us that she remembered the Amish. She said it was a sad day in the Nowata community when the Amish decided to leave. Whether or not they realized it, the Amish, with their quiet manner, integrity, neighborliness, and forthright manner, had been noted and remembered by the larger community in which they lived, even if they were not "of" it.

++++++

[1] The Amish-Mennonites were somewhat more progressive than the more traditional Old Order Amish, though still clearly Amish in basic belief and practice. Among other things, they conducted worship services in a church building rather than in homes. Amish Mennonites in the midwest would later form a conference and still later affiliate with the Mennonite Church.

[2] As mentioned in the Preface, this is the same young woman to whom my paternal great-grandfather, Dan Yoder, was said to have proposed marriage. When she asked for time to think about it, Dan turned and married someone else, opening the way for Fannie, later, to go to Kansas as a housekeeper for the Nisly men. Over his lifetime, Dan would marry four times. It is said that in later life, Dan apologized to Eli for treating Fannie as he did. Curiously, he did not appear to have apologized to Fannie herself.

[3] To be "chosen by "lot" was to have been named by members of the congregation through a secret nominating process and then chosen from among the nominees through a "blind" process believed to

be an expression of God's choice. Ministers so chosen were not seminary trained and, additionally, were "bi-vocational"—meaning they had to support themselves as well as fulfill the duties of "minister."

[4] It was a custom among the Amish for children to take the first letter of their father's name as the middle initial of their own, thus distinguishing members of the community who might share both first and last names. John Yoder thus became John D. Yoder because his father's first name was Daniel.

[5] In the Amish tradition, a young person became independent (or "of age") and could make their own decisions—financially and otherwise—when they turned 21.

[6] John D's father, Daniel, would be widowed three times and would eventually marry a fourth time—this time to a widow, Miriam Hershberger Mullet, who had 11 living children of her own from the previous marriage. Altogether, the "blended" (?) family included 22 living children, though some were already married and had left home by the time Daniel and Miriam were married.

[7] John's half-brother Leo once said that if John had been as good at managing his finances as he was at working with people, he would have been a rich man

[8] The family narrative tells how their neighbors and members of the Amish community bought the animals and the farm equipment at the bank auction and then simply left them in place for John D to continue using.

[9] Years later, a cousin, writing about the Nowata Amish community, picked up on this seemingly contradictory theme in a piece for *Christian Living* magazine entitled "The Lean Years of Prosperity." The magazine is no longer published, but archived copies may be found. See: Haskins, W. (1968). "The Lean Years of Prosperity." *Christian Living.*

Abbreviated Nisly-Yoder Family Tree

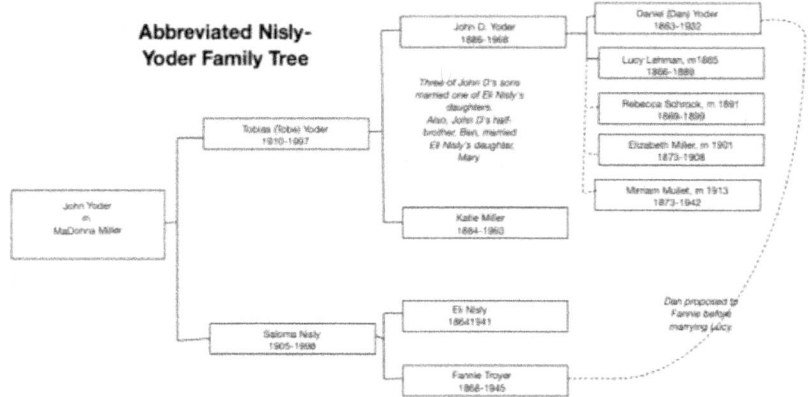

**Abbreviated Nisly-
Yoder Family Tree**

John Yoder
m.
MaDonna Miller

Tobias (Tobe) Yoder
1910-1997

Saloma Nisly
1905-1998

John D. Yoder
1886-1968

Three of John D's sons
married one of Eli Nisly's
daughters.
Also, John D's half-
brother, Ben, married
Eli Nisly's daughter,
Mary

Katie Miller
1884-1960

Eli Nisly
1864-1941

Fannie Troyer
1868-1945

Daniel (Dan) Yoder
1883-1932

Lucy Lehman, m1885
1866-1889

Rebecca Schrock, m. 1891
1869-1899

Elizabeth Miller, m 1901
1873-1908

Miriam Mullet, m 1913
1873-1942

Dan proposed to
Fannie before
marrying Lucy

Part III: Turnings

> ...And both that morning equally lay
> In leaves no step had trodden black.
> Oh, I kept the first for another day!
> Yet knowing how way leads on to way,
> I doubted if I should ever come back.
> — Robert Frost from: *The Road Not Taken*

In the grand arc of a life, the roads taken are defined by their hinge points—the turnings: some hardly noticed, some consequential. The direction of a life becomes, in the end, the sum total of the turnings—those taken and those not taken.

{ five }

Wilderness Interlude

It was one of those perfect late summer days in Canada's northern lake country: a perfectly blue sky mirrored in a glassy, smooth lake; aspens, birches, and evergreens on the far shore dividing the blue of the sky from its mirrored image in the lake below. From somewhere around the point, a small animal, or maybe it was a fish, made a series of small splashes. Oblivious to my presence, a loon landed noisily less than 50 yards from my canoe. I had paddled alone to one of my favorite coves on the far end of the lake, and now, resting my paddle on the bow, I tried to take it all in once again.

In a few days, I'd be heading out on the mail plane, one of the float planes that ferried mail, supplies, and people between the town of Red Lake, some 90 air miles to the south, and the remote boarding school where I had been volunteering for the past two years. My parents and younger sister had driven up from Virginia and were now at Red Lake waiting to be flown in to Poplar Hill for a couple of days. I'd be able to show them something of the world I'd lived in for the past two years. Then I'd join them for the drive home.

Despite the isolation and the challenges of communicating[1] with the outside world, my time at Poplar Hill felt good. I had come to embrace the setting, and I had learned to know and work with people whose views of the world were completely different than mine. I had been asked to do things I had never thought I could do. I had encountered and learned to appreciate—if not to fully understand—a culture and world view that had little in common with the one in which I had been nurtured. I had also made some significant life decisions, with all of the uncertainties that such decisions bring.

Now, in the stillness of the cove at the far end of the lake, wavelets splashing softly against the sides of the canoe, the past, the present, and the future all seemed somehow to collide in a kind of grand mash-up. To my 22-year-old brain, the two years at Poplar Hill seemed like a long time, but, paradoxically, they seemed to have passed in a kind of blurry flash, and I wasn't at all sure that I wanted it to end. My role and my work at the school had been clearly defined; I knew what was expected and believed that I had done it well. Leaving would mark, for me, the end of an era, bringing to an end my first foray into independence. The future looked exhilarating and at the same time, frighteningly unknown.

The decades of the '60s and '70s in the United States were tumultuous and divisive. President John Kennedy, his brother Robert, and Martin Luther King had been assassinated; our country was at war in Vietnam, and the "Catonsville Nine" would be arrested for burning draft records in a parking lot in Catonsville,[1] Maryland. In the spring of 1970, four students were shot by the National Guard at Kent State University. Living as they did, without radio or TV, the Amish community in which I lived during those years had a general awareness of the times, but for the most part, this was all happening out there and had little direct impact on "us."

Still, that was the world in which I, like all Americans, was to a greater or lesser extent, embedded. That world became more concrete when I turned 18 and needed to register for the military draft. The Amish, of course, object to war in all its forms, and it was taken for granted that I would apply to be classified as a Conscientious Objector, a provision that, if granted, would allow me to serve for two years in an approved job that "contributed to the national good" in lieu of military service.

Accordingly, with some assistance from one of our ministers, I wrote a letter to the local Selective Service Board explaining my position against war and requesting to be classified as a Conscientious Objector (CO). In due course, I was summoned to a hearing before the Board. The questions seemed perfunctory, but a few weeks later, the Board followed their own precedent and issued a letter and a draft card classifying me as '1-O'[3] (available for civilian work contributing to the maintenance of the national health, safety, or interest). The Board had been dealing with the Amish for some years and knew some of the families personally; they respected the Amish even if they didn't agree with them. Though my decision to register as a conscientious objector was made without seriously considering alternatives, it was, I believe, the right one for me at that time.[4] I've since come to see participation in the military as a far more complex set of issues than I could have understood as an 18-year-old Amish farm boy.

I don't know whether or not I would actually have been drafted, as the Selective Service at that time used a lottery system that was based on one's birthday. But I had decided that I would, in any case, volunteer to do two years of civilian service as provided by the Draft Board's classification. Volunteering for a service placement not only preempted the draft but also offered an opportunity to serve others in some way while also offering a legitimate way to emancipate, of sorts, from my parental home and my community of origin.

Locations for doing service had to be chosen from among organizations that had been pre-approved by the Selective Service, but I had a couple of criteria of my own, though perhaps not clearly articulated, even to myself. First, for some reason, I wanted it to be something more or less unique to me, something that not "everybody else" was doing. That immediately closed off several options that to me seemed completely uninteresting, such as working at one of our church-related nursing homes or as a hospital attendant. I briefly considered applying for an assignment to do relief work in post-war Europe[5] under the Mennonite Central Committee (MCC). But I knew of several young Amishmen who had recently done that, which took away some of its luster for me. And—inexplicably to me now—Europe just didn't seem that interesting.

Second, while I wanted my assignment to serve others in some way genuinely, I also wanted an assignment that I would find inherently interesting. A few years earlier, I had, more or less by accident, discovered writing by outdoorsman and wilderness guide Sigurd Olson [6] in our local library. I was fascinated by his accounts of canoeing, trekking, and camping in the lakes region of Northern Minnesota and Canada. So, when I discovered an opportunity to volunteer with an organization that worked in isolated "Indian" (now First Nations) communities in northwestern Ontario, it caught my attention. This was the country that Olson had loved and had written about so effectively.

The organization was called the Northern Light Gospel Mission (NLGM), with headquarters in Red Lake, a mining town in Northwestern Ontario, some 250 miles north of the US-Canada border—literally at the end of the road. Traveling deeper into the interior was by bush plane. I learned that NLGM had a boarding school for First Nation students near the small fishing village of Poplar Hill, about 90 miles by air directly north of Red Lake—some 45 minutes by plane. I also learned that, despite being located in Canada, the NLGM was approved by the American Selective Service for Civilian Service through a seconding arrangement with the Mennonite Central Committee (MCC), a recognized service and relief organization of the Mennonite Church. I applied to MCC and, through them, to NLGM, for a position at the school and was accepted, with a stipulation that my actual assignment would be determined after I arrived. It was agreed that I would arrive in late August, shortly before the beginning of the fall school term.

I was to travel by Greyhound bus from Staunton, the nearest bus station to Stuarts Draft, to International Falls, Minnesota, where NLGM had a branch office on the American side of the border. I would stay there until someone from the head office at Red Lake could pick me up. The bus left Staunton in the wee hours of the morning, heading north. A close friend drove me to the station. I remember reaching through the open bus window and gripping his hand as the bus pulled away. The year was 1964; I would celebrate my 21st birthday in about two months.

I spent a couple of nights in International Falls before being picked up by someone from NLGM headquarters for the drive to Red Lake. Red Lake, Ontario, was (and still is) a small town that owes its existence to the discovery of gold nearby, triggering what was said to be the last gold rush in North America in 1925. The town boasted a scattering of wood-frame houses and a handful of small businesses. There were a few sidewalks along the main streets and several docks along the lake where bush planes could be loaded and unloaded to ferry people and supplies into the interior. NLGM's headquarters were a two-story wooden structure situated between the lake and a dock on one side and the town's main street on the other.

It was late on a Saturday afternoon when we arrived at NLGM headquarters. I was told I would stay at Red Lake over the weekend and be flown to Poplar Hill School on Monday. There was a tradition at NLGM headquarters that staff and visitors eat their noon meal together on Sundays. I was, of course, included, though not sure whether I was staff or still a visitor. Two young women volunteers, staff at NLGM's children's home in Red Lake, cooked and served the meal that Sunday. One of them caught my eye. I had no idea, then, that within a few days she would also be assigned to Poplar Hill School and that, over the next two years she and I would spend considerable one-on-one time together (despite rules against school staff dating each other) nor that, some four years later, she and I would be married. But all of that's a different part of the story.

The flight to Poplar Hill on Monday was exciting for this Amish farm boy. I had never flown before, and the (to me trackless) landscape of lakes and bush was entrancing. Our plane, a Cessna 180 on floats,[7] flew low enough for Ralph, one of NLGM's seasoned bush pilots, to point out details as we flew. Near the shore of a lake, he pointed out a moose standing in shallow water feeding on lily pads, apparently unimpressed by the noisy bird flying overhead.

The flights between the school and headquarters carried mail, freight, and, as needed, passengers. Since the regular passenger seats took up extra space and weight, passengers sat on improvised seats. I was securely strapped in, seated atop a case of, as best I can recall, cold cereal. I was to learn from experience that the mailbag, carried to and from Red Lake on such flights, would be our main connection to the outside world.

Nearing the school, Ralph did a fly-by before circling back to land. From the air, we could see the campus situated on a point, across the channel from the nearby First Nations village of Poplar Hill. The cluster of wooden, white painted buildings that made up the campus stood out against the birch and poplar trees, already showing signs of fall color, and the darker evergreens behind them. There was a classroom building, a dormitory, and several houses for staff. There was a dock for boats and float planes where freight was loaded or unloaded. On the hillside overlooking the rest of the campus was a large wooden building, still under construction, that would soon become a new student dormitory. On the far end of the point, there was a small sawmill and, next to it, a generator house for the diesel engine that drove the generator supplying several hours of electricity to the campus each day. (One's ears eventually tuned out the continuous putt-putt of the diesel when it was running. It was only when it stopped unexpectedly that one suddenly "heard" it in its absence!)

I was met on the dock by Aiden, a volunteer from Ohio, who was in charge of freight and greeting new arrivals. I was told I would stay in the staff dormitory for a few nights but would soon be moved to a room in the new, partially finished student dormitory building. My room, next to what would become the boys' dorm, would be my bedroom and "office" for the next two years. The only furniture in the room was a single bed, freshly built from unpainted lumber that had been sawn at the school's sawmill. I would need to build a desk, chair, and any other furniture I might want in the school's shop using lumber[8] from the sawmill. My head was spinning that night as I tried to sleep while trying to wrap my head around the world into which I had just descended, literally, "from above."

I soon met Clair, the principal who would, over the next months, be my boss and my sometime mentor. Clair was a high-energy person with a vision and deep commitment to serving the First Nations people. Sometimes thoughtful, sometimes impulsive, always generous, Clair and I would share significant experiences in the months to come.

Poplar Hill Boarding School, as I would learn, served children of First Nations families who lived in widely scattered villages across the remote lake country of Northwestern Ontario. The Canadian government provided small monthly stipends to most First Nations families, but most of the school's families supplemented their government stipends by fishing, trapping, and selling furs and fish to the local Hudson's Bay trading post, which shipped them out by bush plane. Many families lived in remote fishing or trapping camps for several months of the year without provision for their children's schooling. For these parents, enrolling their children in Poplar Hill offered an attractive option since the Canadian government would pay the tuition. The students lived at the school for each of two semesters, returning home to be with their families for a few weeks over Christmas and during the summer months. Many of these students had already missed some years of schooling, so by the time they came to Poplar Hill, they were older than typical Canadian or American elementary school students. Like other boarding schools for children of indigenous families, Poplar Hill followed the Canadian government curriculum.[9]

My initial assignment was to supervise the boys' dormitory and, while the boys were in school, do campus maintenance. During my second year, I was assigned, in addition, to teach Shop One (carpentry and outboard motor mechanics) to the upper-level boys. It was a hands-on curriculum in which, among other things, students, working in pairs, took apart, and then reassembled, a small outboard motor (Final exam: the motor must run after being put back together!) and, as a class, build a small house that (in this case) would be occupied by a couple or a small family. Building the house involved having the boys clear the site, taking them into the bush to cut logs, building a boom[10] to float the logs to the school's sawmill, then teaching them to (safely) operate the sawmill that would transform the logs into "lumber"[11] before the actual construction could begin.

Before coming to Poplar Hill, I had never even used an outboard motor, much less taken one apart, and my experience as a builder was limited to being an occasional carpenter's helper during slow times on the farm. I knew nothing of running a sawmill. But, somehow, it all came together: the reassembled outboard motors (eventually) ran, and the house we built became the home of a teacher and his family. Not only did I learn something about small outboard motors and building construction, but I learned from others—both students and colleagues—a great deal about myself and about how to manage projects and accomplish team goals.

Only in hindsight, it seems, did I realize how dangerous some of our work was; at the time, no one seemed to give it much thought. The sawmill, for example, could be lethal if proper protocols were not followed. Then, there was the time while the boys and I were in the woods cutting logs for their house project, that a falling tree limb fell directly onto my head, knocking me down and breaking my glasses. We had just felled a tree—with everyone standing well back, out of harm's way we thought. What we didn't see was that some of the branches of the tree we had just felled were intertwined with the one next to it. When the cut tree fell, its branches broke off the intertwined ones from the adjacent tree, which then fell straight down where no one was watching. The limb hit me without warning, leaving me dazed on the ground. But after a few moments, the boys helped me up and we carried on—much as if nothing had happened—though I had to get along without glasses. (That accident is not, apparently, uncommon among greenhorn loggers. Seasoned loggers call it the widow maker.) Then there was the time a slip of the chainsaw took a small notch of skin and bone from just under my right kneecap. It didn't bleed much, and there wasn't much pain, so we just carried on. In the end, my class and I finished the year still alive and generally unscathed.

The boys and I camped in the woods when we were out logging. I learned from them how to make a bannock (a kind of skillet bread) over an open fire and how to create the world's best fish sandwich by wrapping a thick slice of buttered, homemade bread around a fresh-caught walleye fillet, still sizzling from the skillet. Best of all were the stories they shared and the conversations we had around the campfires, where I came face to face, for the first time, with a world and a worldview that challenged the one I had grown up with in rural Virginia. They told of life in the villages and stories they had heard from their parents and the village elders: stories of how the world came to be, stories of animals and trees that could feel and that had voices; stories of spirits that lived in the forests—some friendly and some not so. It was a strange and, to me, inexplicable world that made me question the basis of my own notions about "how the world works." Whether or not the boys accepted the elders' views of the world at face value was unclear; the stories were usually told as something believed by others, but it seemed clear from their telling that they could not dismiss them out of hand, either, nor, by the same token, could I. The boys struggled to integrate the world of their elders with the modern world of their textbooks. But for me, the boys offered windows into paradoxical worlds that I couldn't understand and that were far removed from those of my Amish heritage.

The Northland taught the importance of obeying simple, common-sense rules for survival in an environment that didn't leave room for many mistakes. Sometimes those lessons were taught the hard way. There was, for example, the time Clair and I went moose hunting. Moose meat from the bush was an important part of the diet at the school, and each year the staff (mostly the men) tried to take as many as their licenses would allow. A typical hunting technique was to scout a likely area by ski plane and, when a possible quarry was spotted, land some distance away from sight and stalk the moose on foot. If the hunt was successful, it also meant field dressing the moose and cutting it into pieces that could be packed out to where they could be loaded onto the plane—not a trivial task, as a moose can weigh as much as 1500 pounds!

The trip with Clair didn't actually begin as a moose hunt. He had proposed taking me to Sandy Lake, a "nearby" reserve ("only" an hour or so by plane!) for a kind of cultural exposure visit. Clair was a pilot[12] and sometimes had access to a small, two-seater plane—a Taylor Craft, known as a T-Craft. He proposed to fly me up to Sandy Lake, leave me there for a few days, before returning to pick me up. I welcomed the opportunity. The actual weekend when we would do this depended, as always, on good weather.[13] It was late on a Friday afternoon when we decided the trip was a go for the next day.

The sun was just coming up the following morning as we made our way across the frozen lake to the parked plane; a thick covering wrapped around the engine cowling to keep the oil from congealing. It was cold, probably well below zero (Fahrenheit), but the air was invigorating; the early sky a deep blue—all promising a beautiful, clear, but cold, winter day. Neither Clair nor I had yet filled our moose license that year, and after several minutes in the air, Clair suggested[14] that, since there was plenty of time for us to arrive at Sandy Lake, we could take some time to do some moose hunting. I agreed and we circled slowly over several lakes for a couple of hours, but it wasn't until nearly noon that we spotted a moose standing near an island.

Landing on the opposite side of the island, we began the stalk, making our way over dead-falls and thick underbrush, all hidden under hip-deep snow. Finally, spotting our quarry and getting into position, both of us fired. The animal stumbled but then ran into the bush. We followed the trail and eventually found the moose where it had fallen; a huge bull, likely weighing well over a thousand pounds. Now it needed to be field-dressed—a messy and laborious project at best, but made more complicated in this case by the fact that the moose had more or less collapsed on its stomach onto some dead-falls and needed to be rolled over—a significant task for a creature of that size. Since we hadn't planned for moose hunting, we had to make do with the knives and tools we had at hand for field dressing,

Our process was slow, and as the afternoon wore on, we became aware of a shift in the weather. A whiteout—a snow squall with almost zero visibility—was making its way toward us, and in a short time, we were completely engulfed. There was nothing to do but hunker down and wait it out. The whiteout didn't last more than an hour or so, but by that time it was too dark to fly. Our only choice was to spend the night as best we could, where we were: in deep snow, in sub-zero weather, and many miles from the nearest human habitation.

One of the cardinal rules of bush flying is that whenever possible, one must leave some version of a flight plan—usually verbal, often by radioing a base—giving place and time of departure and the destination so that appropriate action could be taken in case the flight didn't arrive as expected. I learned later that Clair had neglected to do that before leaving Poplar Hill. And since the T-Craft didn't carry a radio, we couldn't notify anyone that we were hunting nor—more importantly—could we tell anyone of our current predicament. First rule: broken. Technically, we were not missing since Poplar Hill had no reason to believe we had not arrived at Sandy Lake, and since Sandy Lake wasn't expecting us, they couldn't raise an alarm when we didn't show up.

A second cardinal rule is that bush planes should always carry a basic survival kit that includes, as a minimum, an ax, sleeping bags, matches, and some canned or dried food. Taking stock of our situation, we found matches and a few tins of food, but only one sleeping bag—and no ax. As it had happened, sometime earlier, oil had gotten onto the sleeping bag that had been in the T-Craft, and the bag had to be discarded. Knowing that I had a personal sleeping bag, Clair had asked if he could borrow it for the T-Craft until he could get a replacement. I agreed, but pointed out that it was only a mild-weather bag, not a cold-weather one. "Never mind," he had said. "It will soon be spring, and the bag should be fine." That was now the sleeping bag inside of which the two of us would somehow have to spend a sub-zero night.

We made our way to a cove that offered some shelter, gathered some "hand wood" (wood that could be broken up without an ax), and started a fire. For dinner, we shared a can of pork and beans. Somehow, we managed to shoehorn both of us, still in our cold-weather outerwear, into my sleeping bag. I am not a large person, but Clair was "portly." It was hardly a comfortable night—but we managed; taking turns during the night to get up and replenish the fire. Morning dawned bright, clear, and cold; another beautiful day for flying. The moose we had shot, now mostly frozen, was still on the far side of the island and only partly field-dressed. It also needed to be quartered so that it could be packed out to be picked up by plane—a labor-intensive process that would be better done with more help. Since the T-Craft was too small to carry cargo in any case, Clair decided that he would fly to Pikangikum, a village southeast of Poplar Hill, and, Clair figured, some 30 minutes by air. He could radio Poplar Hill and Red Lake from there and pick up someone from there to help pack out the meat. He would also request Red Lake to send one of the Cessnas the next day to carry out the meat. Meanwhile, I would stay, finish dressing out the moose (something I'd never done before), and begin packing out the meat. He would be back, Clair assured me, in a few hours at most.

I watched him take off with misgivings, but there wasn't much choice. I returned to the partially field-dressed and now mostly frozen moose and did my best to complete the task. But as the sun passed noon and Clair hadn't returned, I began to feel uneasy. Earlier that morning, I had heard and then seen a plane overhead. At first, I thought it was Clair, but it turned out to be a different plane, flying low and nearby, and then, out of hearing, it was probably a couple of moose hunters from Red Lake. But when, after some time, the plane again began circling near me, in some mounting anxiety about Clair not having returned, I decided to try waving it down. I moved out onto the open lake and waved both arms over my head, hoping they would see me. They did, circling me a time or two and then landing nearby. (It wasn't every day that one found a lone human on a remote, frozen lake.) I explained the situation, and after some head-scratching, we agreed that they would hunt in the area for a while longer but return to check on me before they left.

An hour or so later, I again heard a plane—judging by the sound, a smaller one this time. It was Claire. He circled and landed, but instead of taxing over to where I was, the engine shut down and the plane stopped some distance away. Making my way across the ice to the plane, I found Clair looking shaken. The throttle control had just come off in his hand! The engine could no longer be controlled; the T-Craft was not flyable!

It was a relief, to say the least, when the hunters from Red Lake came back as promised, only to find us with a disabled plane. After the discussion, it was agreed that Clair and I would fly back to Red Lake with them. The fellow from Pikangikum who had returned with Clair, this time better prepared, agreed to stay the night alone and finish packing out the partially butchered moose. He would be picked up, along with the meat, by an NLGM Cessna the next day. Later that winter, when one of the cooks complained about a batch of moose meat that had an "off" flavor, I didn't have the nerve to suggest that I might know something about it.

In the summer of my last year at Poplar Hill, the Canadian government decided to upgrade its support of the government day school at Poplar Hill village across the channel from the Poplar Hill Boarding School. They would, among other things, build a new teacherage—a house for teachers. NLGM was offered the contract to build the house, and I was asked, having just finished the shop-house on campus with my students, to supervise the construction. A few of my former shop students stayed on to help with the construction, along with a few workers from Poplar Hill village. We finished the job in record time, and in my eyes, the project seemed to have gone well. We were commended for a job well done.

One's experiences are, I believe, always embedded in the particulars of place. My two years in the remote bush country of Poplar Hill were no exception. I spent hours fishing, hiking, canoeing or, in winter, snowshoeing—sometimes with buddies or with a group, sometimes alone. It was a world not easily described by words: paddling slowly along a shoreline in early-morning mist and being startled by the black bulk of a moose so near you could almost touch it; the maniacal laughter of a loon at sunset; solitude that wasn't lonely; the crackling silence of a bright blue, sub-zero morning on a snow-covered lake. Or, in a different mood, cutting a perfect "v" with a power boat on a mirror-smooth lake early in the morning, leaving behind a frothy wake like the contrail of a jet plane. Others have said it, but I came to agree: the wilderness has a deep language that speaks if one learns to listen.

And then, there were the people. Poplar Hill School relied heavily on volunteers to teach in its classrooms and keep the school functioning. Many of the volunteers were of similar ages and enjoyed doing things together. There were hikes, canoe trips, fishing, and (fresh!) fish-fries, late evening softball (one could be playing softball at 10:00 or 11:00 pm in summer) or, in winter, table games. Sometimes, staff put on informal concerts or plays for the students. Coming, as they did, from a variety of places and with a variety of backgrounds, the staff exposed me to different ways of thinking and doing. Some of the friendships lasted after leaving the school. It was hardly an accident that, despite rules against staff "dating" (an unpopular, but not un-reasonable rule, given the setting), several of the staff would get married to each other after leaving the school.

MaDonna and I became "friendly" soon after we arrived at Poplar Hill. We had some parallel responsibilities—she with the girls and I with the boys—and we sometimes worked together. We discovered common interests: a love of the outdoors, hiking, canoeing, snowshoeing, and quieter activities, such as playing table games, ping-pong, or just talking. We agreed to write when I left after two years.

But there was another, deeper dimension. Like the Amish worldview and the taken-for-granted traditions in which I had been encul-turated, the students who came to us at Poplar Hill were similarly embedded within the traditions, folkways, and legends of their own culture. They had inherited the worldview of the First Nations peoples. They could read the behavior of animals from their tracks, tell directions from the stars, find their way home through what seemed like trackless wilderness, and predict the weather by "smelling the wind." But it was also, for them, a world of mystery, where the trees and the animals had voices and were populated by spirits—spirits that sometimes behaved in unpredictable, even unfriendly, ways and that sometimes must be placated. Wisdom resided with the ancient ones and was conveyed in the legends and stories told by their parents and the tribal elders.

We taught them about the contemporary—i.e., white, western—ways of the world. We taught them to read books, to conduct scientific experiments, and to believe that the natural world could be explained if one understood its laws. They accepted our teachings, and most did well on the exams we gave them. But the world of their parents and of the ancient ones was still with them, and sometimes that world collided with the one we taught inside the classroom walls. And we, schooled as we were in the traditions of the scientific and industrial revolutions, had no satisfactory answers about how to bring those worlds into alignment.

In a few days, I would leave all of this behind, making my way into still other worlds about which I knew next to nothing. The sadness at leaving this complicated but pristine world mingled with anticipation and apprehension about what lay ahead. For the past two years, I'd been living in a cocoon of sorts, a world that had taken on its own substance and meaning and that had almost no connection to the one I'd lived in before. Could worlds so different even exist in the same universe—or in the same person?

++++++

[1] Sometimes the mail plane, our primary means of contact with the outer world, made a couple of trips a week; sometimes, during bad weather or during spring "breakup" or fall "freezeup," it could be weeks between trips. There was no airstrip; planes either flew with skis or floats, depending on the season.

[2] There was no way I could have known it back then, but many years later, when MaDonna and I retired, we ended up in Catonsville! There is now a plaque commemorating the event and the spot. A Little League baseball team in Catonsville now calls itself the "Catonsville Nine."

[3] 1-O classification is officially defined as a "Conscientious objector available for civilian work contributing to the maintenance of the national health, safety, or interest." When one was in an approved work assignment, the classification was changed to 1-W.

[4] As an 18-year-old Amish boy I had little understanding of the complexities underlying these questions.

[5] There were still relief and rebuilding projects going on in Europe into the '50s and '60s.

[6] Years later, I was surprised to find that his books were still in print. Olson's writing, I found, could still strike a similar chord

as they did with a 17-year-old Amish lad. Perhaps it was his ability to capture and communicate his deep love of the natural world and the out-of-doors; perhaps it was his ability to invite me to imagine a world different from any I'd ever experienced.

[7] The floats would be exchanged for skis when the lakes froze over then changed back to floats during spring "break-up.

[8] For the first few months, the walls consisted of heavy "Kraft Paper" stapled to the 2x4 studding while we waited until hardboard paneling could be brought in by a "tractor train" over the frozen lakes. The train consisted of several heavy sledges pulled by a cater-pillar tractor. The crew had to break trail through the bush and across the frozen lakes under rigorous conditions. They cooked and slept in a kind of "caboose" that was the last sled of the train. The trip from Red Lake to Poplar Hill took days of "very tough sledding" in sub-zero weather.

[9] As a twenty-year-old Amish farm boy, I had no inkling of how the well-meaning but seriously misguided policies for teaching and discipline that were common practice among Canadian residen-tial schools in those years were harmful to the students they were intended to help. While I believe Poplar Hill avoided the most atro-cious of the practices that came to light in the following decades, the school was guided, as were most other Canadian residential schools, by the (mistaken) belief that teaching children to speak, think and act like "white people" was the best way to ensure that they had a chance to succeed in life. It is important, I think, to acknowledge the harm that was done. The Canadian government established a Truth and Reconciliation Commission in 1982 to investigate the schools and to recommend responses. The Commission's report is available online.

[10] Logs were taken from the bush to the sawmill by being dragged into a lake and encircled by logs fastened together in a kind of chain forming a "boom." The boom would be slowly dragged by an

outboard-powered boat to the sawmill. Keeping the boom intact and chasing down logs that had escaped was a continual challenge.

[11] Because fresh-cut lumber needed a year or more to dry before it could be used in construction, we actually stacked the lumber we cut for use in next year's project. The previous year's class had sawed the lumber we used for the house we built.

[12] Clair's wife, Clara, who often flew with Clair, had also gotten her pilot's license because, she said, she wanted to be able to land the plane, she said, in case something happened to Clair while in the air.

[13] Since all bush flights were by visual flight rules, the weather was a major factor in determining whether or not planes could safely fly on any given day.

[14] I suspect that Clair may have had this in mind all along.

{ six }

"Higher" Education

They were still there, just as I remembered them: the Blue Ridge Mountains, some 2800 feet above sea level and just a few miles from my parents' front porch. From the porch, I could see changes in the valley: a housing development on the other side of the river, a manufacturing plant near the tracks, but the mountains were still there, a kind of bulwark against change. But maybe that was an illusion. I was no longer the same person who had left Stuarts Draft two years ago—and the world I was seeing was no longer the same either. I had just returned late the evening before from two years at the remote Poplar Hill School. My parents and my younger sister had driven to Red Lake to pick me up. But after two years away, coming back to Stuarts Draft seemed surreal. The familiar landmarks, the places I knew like the back of my hand, were still there and mostly unchanged. But I hadn't thought about them for two years; now I seemed to be seeing them for the first time. Everything was smaller, less relevant, and more distant; it was "home"—but somehow it wasn't.

In a couple of weeks, I'd be enrolling as a 22-year-old freshman at Eastern Mennonite College, some 30 miles up the road from Stuarts Draft. I had only the sketchiest of ideas about what that would entail, but it would be a new chapter. I had no maps for the uncharted roads.

The Amish do not, of course, approve of education beyond the minimum required by law, so the decision to attend college is tantamount to a decision to leave the Amish church. But there were, among my Amish relatives and acquaintances, a few who had earned a bachelor's degree and had become teachers or, less often, gone on to become medical doctors—my brother[1] Leo among them. Some of the conservative Mennonites,[2] many of whom had Amish roots, came to accept the necessity of a college degree if one were to become a qualified teacher (preferably to teach in a church-related school) or a doctor (mainly to become a missionary doctor). Even among those who left the Amish for higher education, there were few, if any, role models for any professions or careers besides teaching or medicine (nursing if you were female).

I don't know when I first began thinking that I would attend college. But somewhere during my teen years, what had begun as a question ("Would I?") morphed into an assumption, and the questions changed from "whether" to "when and how?" I don't think either my parents or my siblings were surprised at my decision. By that time, Leo was in his final year of medical school and had thus already broken through the higher education ceiling in our family. Even though he was ten years my senior, and because of that we didn't share many experiences, I admired him greatly and he became a model for me to emulate, short of going into medicine myself. Somehow, I felt the need to be different.

I don't remember discussing the decision to go to college with my parents, though I'm sure I did. While that likely would not have been the future they would have chosen for me, they respected the choices both Leo and I had made. Even though there was much they didn't understand and even though our experiences lay far outside the boundaries of the worlds in which they had grown up, they were interested and supportive of us as their sons. Though their Amish "humility" would have kept them from saying it, I believe they were, in fact, quite "proud" (in an Amish kind of way) of us both. My parents didn't attend my college graduation. I'm sure I invited them, though I don't specifically remember doing it. I believe they were pleased at my success, but both I and they understood that the world of colleges and higher education was outside of their comfort zone.

By today's standards, I would no doubt have been classified as culturally, educationally, and economically "disadvantaged": I was a high school dropout, was not familiar with mainstream culture, and had no money. (Not that such a classification would have made much difference then. Few colleges and universities recognized the disadvantaged as a category in those days, and there were few, if any, programs to offer them special support. I didn't actually consider myself to be disadvantaged, though—perhaps because I didn't know what I didn't know. It was also true that while I lacked some of the important knowledge, experiences, and resources some of my classmates had, I had other advantages that, in some ways at least, more than compensated.

It was during my last year at Poplar Hill School that the decision to try enrolling in college became concrete. I don't remember consulting or discussing it with anyone in particular at Poplar Hill, though I must have. Conveniently, my assignment at Poplar Hill ended near the end of the summer, so I reasoned I could transition directly into the fall semester. I could, in other words, go straight from two isolated years in the Canadian bush almost straight onto a college campus. I hadn't really thought of it in those terms and probably wasn't really prepared for the shock.

It was more or less my foregone conclusion that my college of choice would be Eastern Mennonite College (now Eastern Mennonite University) in Harrisonburg, Virginia. Harrisonburg was just some 30 miles from Stuarts Draft, and I had some sense of familiarity with it. It had been Leo's alma mater (though he never graduated; he was accepted into medical school without a college degree), and a couple of first cousins had attended there. During my teen years, a few of us from the Stuarts Draft youth group (and who may have been living along the fringes of the church) occasionally drove up to EMC to attend a concert, and cousins who were students sometimes invited us to their dorms. So it felt as though I knew the college, which, given my limited knowledge of other options, helped make it the obvious choice.

During the winter of my last year at Poplar Hill, I wrote to Eastern Mennonite asking for a catalog and about admissions requirements. Some weeks later, the mailbag brought a personal letter from the head of the admissions office saying that I could submit a passing GED score in lieu of a high school diploma and that the college would do its best to put together a financial package for me that was workable. Further, if I could find a qualified and willing proctor, they would mail the GED to Poplar Hill, and I could take it on-site.

I never seriously considered the possibility that I might not pass the GED, though I probably should have. I had been a voracious reader for years, so I expected to do well enough on the general knowledge, language reasoning, and social studies sections, but science and mathematics might be challenging. I understood basic arithmetic, of course, but had only a superficial knowledge of algebra, and my knowledge of science was mostly limited to what I had learned informally about the world of nature. But the college mailed a practice exam to my proctor and I worked my way through that material. Eventually, I decided I was ready and took the exam on a Saturday in one of the Poplar Hill classrooms. Oddly, I never received any information about results from GED or from EMC. The answer, I suppose, came in the form of the letter from EMC that arrived a few weeks later offering me admission, along with a generous (by the standards of the time) financial package that included substantial work study and student loan components.

Because the regular dorms were full, I was assigned to an off-campus house that had been rented by the college for overflow. Dubbed "Hillside," the house was just over the crest of a hill west of the main campus. The view of the west valley from our living room window was spectacular, and we could easily walk to classes by crossing to the other side of the hill. (Which, as an added bonus, offered a splendid hilltop view of the city and of the Shenandoah Valley in the other direction.) There were 10 college men assigned to the house, ranging from Walter and Paul, senior philosophy and pre-med students respectively, to Larry and Maynard, and me, who were freshmen and mainly just trying to figure out what was going on. It was a good mix and we got on well, but I quickly became aware that the world they had grown up in was very different from mine. I hadn't seen their movies, hadn't listened to their music, or read the books they had discussed in high school. I had never watched a football game or gone to a high school prom.

The informal bull sessions in the house ranged from philosophy to politics to baseball and much more. J.A.T. Robinson's *Honest to God* (apparently assigned reading in someone's class) evoked a great deal of discussion and, for me, personal reflection. Robinson called for going beyond the stock answers and the generally accepted concepts of traditional theology and asking honest questions about one's religious experience. Though I had long questioned Amish beliefs and practices, the dawning realization that it was okay, even important, to allow the questions to go still broader and deeper, came more gradually. Asking honest questions about fundamental beliefs risks undermining and toppling one's entire belief system. Like many others, it was only over time that I came to realize that asking questions honestly—and allowing the answers to go where they may—was the only pathway to a worldview and belief system that was authentically mine. (The follow-on lesson was learned even more gradually and over most of a lifetime: that "honesty" in the name of "truth" can be elusive and multifaceted and would often need to be renegotiated.)

Registering for classes was a confusing hurdle. I came to college with the general idea that I wanted to become a teacher, but had no clear idea what I wanted to teach nor did I even have a clear understanding of the options. Within the first two weeks, I switched my declared major three or four times. (Though I didn't fully understand why, I was sure I didn't want to go into a pre-med major, because that's what Leo had done. I needed to chart my own course.) The proforma responses of the faculty member assigned to advise me were of little help.

Eventually, a plan fell into place. The basic idea came from a fellow freshman, Dave, who had decided he didn't really care all that much about teaching, but wanted to be a guidance counselor. Virginia, at the time, required at least two years of successful classroom teaching followed by a master's degree in counseling in order to become a guidance counselor. What one taught during those two years, Dave observed, didn't really matter so long as one completed them successfully. It was an interesting idea, and I liked the notion of being a Guidance Counselor—though I'd never had one or seen one at work. But, influenced by the writings of John Holt (*How Children Learn* and *How Children Fail*, both published in the '60s), I was also intrigued by observing and trying to understand the mental processes by which children, especially younger ones, learn. So, with encouragement from a faculty mentor in the Education Department, I eventually settled into a major in Elementary Education. It was a kind of open-ended decision from which I could follow "Dave's plan" or stick with the equally intriguing questions around the psychology of learning and just focus on teaching kids. (As it turned out, I was the only one of the two of us who stuck to Dave's plan. Dave's career took off in a different direction altogether.) I also had some notion that I might be able to return to Canada to teach in a reservation school in Northwest Ontario.

Besides my education courses, I took elective classes in literature and writing (and, on the other end of the spectrum, accounting!). I did well enough (I missed making the Dean's List only one or two semesters over my four years of college), but was, again, acutely aware that my classmates came with a set of experiences and knowledge that I didn't have. What felt worse, I hadn't even known how much I didn't know, until my classmates began, for example, talking in familiar terms about authors I'd never even heard of. Some had already published poetry or short stories. I also became aware of economic differences. Though not all students, of course, came from wealthy families, I had a hard time coming to terms with the kid who showed off the flashy new car he'd been given as a high school graduation gift or the one who complained about having to drive his parents' new Mercedes because his was in the shop. I was clearly not "of" the world many of my classmates lived in. (I didn't even own a car until Leo loaned me $300 to buy a 7-year-old Plymouth sedan. It was an ugly car, but it served me well for years.)

Early in my freshman year, I joined a student organization that did off-campus service activities. My group was assigned to help out at a small Mennonite church in the foothills, some 20 miles northwest of campus. It was a connection that lasted throughout my college years. We organized youth activities, taught Sunday school classes, and helped with music. It was a good experience, one that offered connections with other students as well as with the local mountain folk who attended. Technically, I was still Amish since I had not formally left the Amish or joined any other church, though I had already done so "in my head" for some time. So, it was at this simple mountain church that I formalized my departure from the Amish church when, at the conclusion of a Sunday morning service, I was taken in as a member. Though it made little practical difference, it was a significant step of letting go of an old identity.

MaDonna and I had spent time together at Poplar Hill, despite rules prohibiting staff from dating each other (we didn't "date," we just went boating or took walks together)—and when I left, we had agreed to correspond. I returned to Poplar Hill for a visit over my first Christmas break, and she came to Virginia in the summer between my freshman and sophomore years at college. I had a job that summer as an attendant at a state mental hospital, and she took a job as a nursing aid in a local nursing home. Before the summer ended, we became engaged. Given that we were both committed to school schedules and living many miles apart, we set our wedding date for the following summer. We planned to get married in the small church in Oregon where she had grown up, and where her parents and members of her family still attended.

MaDonna returned to Poplar Hill for the school term before traveling to Oregon early the following summer. I finished my 2nd year in college, then joined her in Oregon. (A college friend and I drove my old Plymouth straight through from Virginia to Oregon, stopping only for food and fuel—and a pair of tires. We made the trip in about 30 hours, start to finish. One of us would drive while the other slept on the back seat.) MaDonna's father arranged a summer job for me with the construction company he worked for.

We were married in mid-July in the small, white church in the foothills of Oregon's Cascade Mountains where MaDonna had grown up. It was a quite conservative congregation and we struggled, even just for the summer, to reluctantly conform to their expectations. My parents and my younger sister traveled from Virginia to Oregon for the wedding by train. A college friend who was working as a summer ranger in Yosemite National Park that summer came to Oregon to be the best man. We honeymooned on the Oregon/Washington coast, where we discovered that the Pacific Ocean off the Washington/Oregon Coast felt freezing cold, even in July. Forget about swimming!

A few weeks after the wedding, MaDonna and I piled the sum of our belongings—including a lovely cedar chest that one of her brothers had made some years before—into the back of the Plymouth and headed back east. (We had to remove the rear seat cushion to accommodate the cedar chest.) Returning to Harrisonburg, we rented a tiny basement apartment a short distance from campus. MaDonna began working for a nearby publishing company, and I continued my studies, but now as an off-campus, married student.

In the fall of my senior year, my department distributed application forms for the GRE (Graduate Record Examination). I was, by that time, less certain about the future, and the idea of earning a graduate degree seemed remote now that I was married. Just getting a bachelor's degree had been a major step. But our department encouraged us to take the GRE even if we weren't sure about ever doing graduate work, arguing that it would be good to have GRE scores on record and, further, we'd likely do better on them as senior college students than we would later. I took their advice, registered, and took the exam. (To my surprise, my scores on the GRE were quite high. My Amish upbringing had schooled me well against feeling "proud," but there was no prohibition against being "pleased.") Only later did I realize how pivotal the GRE was to the evolution of my life journey. My advisors in the Education department at EMC were right: having the GRE scores in my portfolio was important.

But despite sometimes feeling like I was in a foreign world, my years at EMC were good ones. I played volleyball, sang in a couple of touring choirs, and made lots of friends and connections, some of which continued long after college. Though I worked for the grades I got, I reveled in most of the coursework, especially those related to psychology. I gradually came to feel more or less at home in that world, even if at other times, I was convinced I could never belong.

With graduation, there was, of course, the business of getting a job. I submitted the usual round of applications to the surrounding school districts. I also applied to Indian Affairs in Canada to teach in a reservation school, but got no response. Clair, my former principal at Poplar Hill, followed up with an inquiry to Indian Affairs on my behalf—he had really hoped I would get a position in one of their schools—and was told they were only hiring Canadian citizens. Meanwhile, I was being recruited by several church-related schools but had been holding them off. But after a particularly persuasive call from a Mennonite K-10 school near Mt. Joy, PA, I accepted. I would teach World Geography and music(!). It was only a short time later that I got a long-distance call from Indian Affairs in Ontario wondering if I was still available to take an open position in one of the reservation[3] schools. Much as I would have liked to accept their offer, I felt bound to honor my commitment to Mt. Joy. Further, MaDonna was by that time pregnant with our first son: clearly, living on a reservation in Northwest Ontario would have been a more complicated environment in which to begin a family! Teaching in a remote, reservation school became a road not taken.

I stayed at the school in Mt. Joy for two years, then left to pursue a master's degree in counseling at the University of Virginia. My two years at Mt. Joy had gone well enough, but I was teaching out of my field, and neither the setting nor the teaching seemed to have found their way to a sweet spot. Anyway, there was the "plan." The Master's in Counseling was a one-year, full-time program. We moved into an apartment in Charlottesville in the summer before the beginning of the semester. I took a short-term job as a finish carpenter with a local builder for a few months before the university's fall term began. Even though our finances were tight, we enjoyed Charlottesville: its cultural opportunities, its tree-lined streets, its parks, and, of course, the University "Grounds" (never "campus!"). A highlight of that year was the birth of our daughter, Karla.

After completing the degree and qualifying for state certification, I accepted a position as a guidance counselor in a junior high school in Virginia's "Southside"—the region extending, roughly, from the south side of the James River to the border with North Carolina. Culturally and demographically, the area had more in common with the Carolinas and the Deep South than with other parts of Virginia. Though it was the same state, the culture and traditions that we encountered in Southside Virginia were nothing like those of my growing-up years in Virginia's Shenandoah Valley.

The decision to pursue doctoral studies some four years later was an obvious determining factor in our family's lives. I still remember the day when the decision was made: something in my head flipped, like an electrical switch, and what had been a kind of lingering question became a decision. I was then in my second year as a principal of an intermediate school in the same district where I had been hired as a guidance counselor.

It had been a gray day with drizzling rain. I'd just finished sitting through the district superintendent's monthly staff meeting. The meeting had dragged on for over two hours, covering a less-than-inspiring agenda: changes in state regulations, new policies on teachers' leave days, pros and cons of new science textbooks, and talk of what we should do to improve test scores. (Not much talk about improving learning, though.)

Our district's schools had been integrated for less than a decade. Like many school districts in the South, the schools for Blacks had, for decades, been chronically under-funded and under-resourced and the effects of those disparities would continue to show up for years, even after the schools were integrated. I believed in what I was doing and felt invested in my work, but now, driving back to my school in the gray, late afternoon drizzle, something clicked: this was not how I wanted to spend the rest of my career. I was thirty-three years old.

I had not sought the principalship that I now held. In my second year as a guidance counselor, I felt reasonably happy. I had been given a lot of freedom to define an interesting blend of tasks and responsibilities. The principal of my school and I were of a similar age, and we got on well together. Still, though the job had been part of my long-range plan of sorts, I had begun wishing for something more intellectually stimulating. One late afternoon, after the students had gone home, the District Superintendent, who happened to be in our building, stopped me in the hall and asked whether I would consider accepting an appointment as principal at one of the district's intermediate schools. The current principal had been reassigned, he said, and they were looking for a replacement who could carry things forward with a steady hand.

I was honored to be asked, but was inclined to say no. Becoming a school principal was on my list of things I had vowed years ago that I would not do. But here it was. I was being affirmed and was being offered what was described as "an opportunity." I knew that the job would be challenging, but I was naive enough to think that I could figure it out even though I had absolutely no experience in the role. So, after some days of wavering, discussion with MaDonna, encouragement by my principal, and arguing with myself, I accepted. I would need to become certified by the state as a principal, but I would have a window of a few years in which to do it. I signed up for one of the required courses that summer.

My work as principal went well enough, though not without its predictable challenges. There was, of course, the "sturm und drang" (storm and stress) of adolescents to deal with, but there were also more intractable issues, such as how to manage a school where long-buried racial and class differences were still smoldering, though rarely talked about. Or, how to deal with a family whose instinctual reaction to conflict was to "just hit back harder?" How does one teach an entire student body—and some of their teachers, for that matter—alternate ways of dealing with conflict? I learned a lot from the experienced faculty who were part of my team. The faculty (and most parents) were generally supportive and patient with me, but had clear ways of signaling when they thought I had made a poor decision.

I was caught off guard, though, by the discovery that, though ostensibly accepted, we were still outsiders in this small, closely knit community. In a way that was strangely reminiscent of the Amish worldview, there was a clear division in their world between "us" and "them." Long-term residents—families who had lived there for at least a generation, if not two—were "us"; the rest, such as myself and our family, were "them." We were treated well enough, but we were not on the other side of an invisible social and cultural line. The line wasn't personal, of course. My administrative assistant at the school, for example, told me that though she and her family had lived in the community for 20 years, they were, and would always be, outsiders. In such small communities, everyone knew everyone, and there was no escaping the invisible label of where you came from and how long you'd been there. Almost everyone understood the nuanced classification system. I was forever grateful to the veteran colleagues who patiently and sensitively guided my understanding of subtle distinctions I would have completely missed.

In a mostly segregated world, they had their own churches and social organizations; they understood each other. They, too, had their own boundary lines defining who, within the Black community, was in and who was not, not to mention the lines between them and the White community. There were, of course, well-to-do members of the Black community, but many were on the opposite end of the economic spectrum. This was brought home to me one summer when the school district hired me to do clean-up census work. The job entailed searching out and going to households that had apparently been missed or had not responded to the regular census. The task took me into back roads and country lanes where I might find an elderly couple or, sometimes, a family, still living in a sharecropper's cabin—sometimes without running water or even, on a few occasions, without electricity. I learned to expect—and respect—the dogs that almost always announced my arrival. I was treated with suspicious politeness, though my ID badge helped explain who I was and why I was there. On a few occasions, the residents refused to call off the dogs or to come to the door, and there was nothing to do but drive off. I was glad when the summer was over, but the insights into this world that was more or less hidden in plain sight were eye-opening. The schools and public places were by then superficially—and by law—integrated, but functionally, many of the old lines were still there. White and Black faculty could work together while at school, but returned to separate worlds in different parts of the town and the county when they left the building.

The idea of going back to graduate school was not a new one, but there had always been questions and reasons for putting off the decision. Chief among them were practical concerns: our second son and third child, Daryl, had been born during our second year of living in Southside. We now had three young children. How could we possibly support our family while I was in graduate school? But driving back to my office on that gray day, the switch had flipped; I would do it! We'd figure it out!

I had been disappointed by what to me felt like softness, scientifically speaking, in my training as a counselor. I had hoped for tools that would peel back more layers of understanding about human behavior. Instead, we focused on developing listening skills and showing, somehow, that we understood. Thinking that clinical psychology might feel like a more scientific approach, I applied to the Clinical Psychology program at the University of Virginia. However, that program was small and highly selective, and I was not accepted. (A school principal becoming a clinical psychologist was hardly a typical career path!) After more exploration, I shifted my focus to a related area that seemed to offer a solid theoretical underlayment: I applied and was accepted into UVA's doctoral program in Educational Psychology, focusing on human learning and development. It was a program that could lead to either (or both) qualification as a licensed school psychologist or to an academic appointment. So, in the late summer of 1977, we moved back to Charlottesville. Our rented brick house--more of a cottage really--was small but attractive, in a solid neighborhood and only a block from the elementary school our two oldest would attend.

I had been accepted into the Ed.D. program in the School of Education. But a couple of months later, I learned that I could transfer to a Ph.D. program in the Graduate School of Arts and Sciences by meeting language and research requirements and by adding someone from the Graduate School of Arts and Sciences to my dissertation committee. On the advice and with the support of my advisor, I switched to the Ph. D. program. The move into the Ph.D. program was, more than I realized at the time, pivotal and a key flexion point, changing the direction of my career. Earning a Ph.D. opened a different set of doors.

Financially, the years of doctoral study were a challenge. I took on part-time work teaching in an adult education program, and MaDonna did child care in our home. But there was never money for anything extra, and I felt pressure to complete my studies as quickly as possible so that I could begin earning a salary once again. I carried a maximum course load and compressed my dissertation research and writing (which MaDonna typed) into as compact a time frame as possible. Though I would have been qualified, I never considered applying for a position with the Charlottesville or Albemarle County school systems; I was not interested in doing doctoral studies part-time. In hindsight, in spite of paper credentials to the contrary, with my rural Amish upbringing, I would no doubt have been poorly positioned to offer "guidance" to children living in the world of well-to-do, professional families that were predominant in that area.

In spite of financial pressures, I enjoyed my doctoral work immensely. Besides the usual graduate student roles as teaching and research assistant, I was invited onto an evaluation team for a major grant, and during my last year, I served as a consultant to medical school faculty on assessment. My fellow students were bright and hardworking; my doctoral advisor insisted on calling me "paragon." (I had to look up the word to see what he meant.) Our family enjoyed living in Charlottesville. The setting offered great opportunities for cultural enrichment and for developing friendships. We became active in the local Mennonite Church, and our two oldest were enrolled in an excellent school. But financial realities forced us to make plans to move on as soon as we could.

I was hoping for an academic position when I finished my doctoral work and applied to several universities nationwide. I interviewed at a few, but nothing concrete emerged. During my final year, the department chair, Jerry, contacted me about an open position at Baylor University, for which a former colleague had notified him. Jerry thought I would be a good fit for it and that I had a good chance of being selected. He encouraged me several times to submit an application, but I couldn't see my way to living in Texas and wasn't very keen about Baylor, so I didn't follow up.[4]

I was still actively in search mode when, one evening, I got a call from Lester, my former advisor and mentor at Eastern Mennonite. He had been following my career and knew that I was finishing up my doctoral studies. Lester had been consulting with a church-related school in central Pennsylvania that was embroiled in conflict between the superintendent and the Board of Trustees. Seeing no resolution, Lester had recommended that both the superintendent and the Chair of their Board resign, which they did. Then, with a new board chair in place, he called me to ask whether I would consider taking the job as superintendent. I thanked him for the call, but said no. I was looking for a different kind of position. But Lester, in his inimitable, soft-spoken, low-key way, persisted. After a few more conversations, along with the pressure I felt to begin earning a salary, I relented and agreed to an interview with the new Board chair. The interview was to be at the school in Belleville. The interview went well, the salary offer was generous, and almost before I knew it, I had agreed to be named Superintendent of the school.

Unsurprisingly, my advisors at the University of Virginia were less than happy with my decision. They had hopes for me as an academic and a researcher. I, too, had mixed feelings, but in the end, the decision felt good. The experience at the school in Belleville turned out to be positive: I was warmly welcomed by the community and supported by the Board of Trustees and the faculty. I enjoyed interacting with the students and their parents, but as time went on, I began to feel restless and think about a transition. As described earlier, some five years after settling into Belleville, we found ourselves on a plane heading to Botswana. Interestingly, less than a week after accepting the position at Belleville, I had gotten a call from the head of a search committee at a state university in the Deep South. They had reviewed my CV and wanted me to come for an interview. I turned them down with mixed feelings. I only realized later how my time at Belleville, besides giving me good leadership experience, led me through doorways that would not otherwise have been opened. We would not have gone to Botswana had we not first gone to Belleville.

++++++

[1] After completing I-W service at a mental hospital, Leo attended Eastern Mennonite College and then the University of Virginia Medical School. As a physician, he served for years in Tanzania and Ethiopia and later as a specialist in Hansen's Disease (leprosy) at Carville, Louisiana. He remained a member of a more progressive Beachy Amish church during his years of training.

[2] "Mainline" Mennonites had established a half-dozen or so colleges across the country early in the 20th century. Often, though not always, those with Amish roots would attend one of the Mennonite colleges.

[3] This, in spite of having said earlier that they were only hiring Canadian citizens. Given later developments in Indian Affairs schools, I've been forever grateful that I didn't accept their invitation.

[4] In the "umpteen" years since then, having vaguely followed developments at Baylor, I'm forever grateful that I didn't land there!

{ seven }

Bo-Tswana

It was late in the afternoon when we decided, on impulse, to drive the short distance from our home in Gaborone to Kgale Hill and, for one last time, climb the rocky trail to the summit. Rising some 4,000 feet above sea level, climbing to the top of Kgale (Setswana for "The Place That Dried Up") was one of our favorites. From the rock shelf at the top, there was a panoramic view of the city with the handful of taller buildings[1] near the center partially encircled by two concentric ring roads with bisecting cross-streets that radiated outward like the spokes of a wheel. Beyond the carefully laid-out center, the farther districts merged into an incoherent maze of neighborhoods lying, cheek by jowl, next to each other. The late afternoon haze, a mixture of smoke and atmospheric fog, hung over the more distant parts. To the right of the city, the water of the Gaborone Dam caught the reflection of the sun dipping toward the horizon. We watched as dusk settled and city lights began blinking on, the low hills on the far horizon gradually disappearing behind a gauzy haze. The sharp barks of a nearby baboon troop told us we were being watched.

It was August, winter in the Southern hemisphere, and the evening air felt colder as we turned and made our way back down to the parking lot. It was the dry season; there had been no rain for months, and our steps raised little puffs of dust. Some months earlier, we'd made the decision to leave this city and the country we'd called home for the past seven years. We'd fly from the new Sir Seretse Khama International[2] Airport, toward destinations in Europe and America, landing eventually in Fresno, California, where I would begin a new position. Had it really been seven years since we'd landed in this land-locked, arid country in southern Africa? We had come here as strangers; now we felt "strangely at home." It was a place and a people that, for all of the quirkiness and contradictions, we'd come to know and love. Leaving wouldn't be easy.

This wasn't the way we had planned it. According to our plan, we would stay in Botswana for two years. That would, we reasoned, be time enough to experience a new country and perhaps visit a few others on our way to and from. But it didn't work out that way. The two years had become four, and the four had become seven. Now we were about to return to the country from which we had come. Superficially, we most likely looked like the same people that had left three-quarters of a decade earlier—though certainly older! But in our minds, we knew better. We didn't realize, even at that time, that the land to which we thought we were returning no longer existed—at least not as we had known it. In actuality, the country probably hadn't changed all that much. But we had.

Those insights, though, would come later. For now, we couldn't help but reflect on the experiences of living in this country about which we had known so little when we first came there.

Dominated by the semi-arid Kalahari Desert, the region that is now Botswana had been, before recorded history, occupied by nomadic hunter-gatherers known as the San (sometimes popularly called Bushmen). Over centuries, the San had perfected the art of living in harmony with the land and its animals and vegetation, leaving behind only a small footprint.[3] But the San had a kind of sophistication of their own. Their skills as trackers and hunters and sheer ability to survive in a harsh land are legendary. They were also remarkable and prolific artists; leaving thousands of rock paintings across their land—still visible—that are believed to be thousands of years old. (The British Museum termed the area "The Louvre of the Desert.")

The Tswana, a subgroup of ethnic Bantu living in Southern Africa, came—relatively speaking—much later, probably between 400 and 600 CE. Though many Tswana live in South Africa, they are, by a considerable margin, the largest ethnic group in Botswana, comprising some 80 percent of the population. The prefix "bo," in the Tswana language, can mean different things depending on context. As part of the name adopted by the country at independence, it can be understood to mean "the land." Thus, Botswana can be translated simply and appropriately as "The Land of the Tswana" or Bo-Tswana. This was the area made famous in 19th-century England by the missionary efforts of Robert Moffat, David Livingstone, and the London Missionary Society.

A representative from the university was at the airport to greet and welcome us when we arrived. Unfortunately, he said, there was no house available for us yet. In the meantime, we would be staying in two rooms at the Gaborone Sun hotel (otherwise known as The Sun) near the University. The University would pay for two hotel rooms and, for the first month, cover the cost of our family's food at the hotel restaurant. The "Sun," we discovered, was a modern, air-conditioned, comfortable hotel. The patio doors in the back of our rooms opened to a large, well-maintained lawn[4] with tennis courts and an Olympic-size swimming pool surrounded by a flagstone deck. There were chaise lounges for sunning. Though it wasn't what we had expected, we adjusted. It was an easy walk to the University, and the kids spent hours at the pool every afternoon after school—and loved being able to order whatever they chose from the menu at the hotel restaurant. (The novelty of being able to order at will from the menu lasted little more than a week. Then it became "But I don't want *that* again!") Some of our earliest friendships were formed around the hotel pool with others who would also be teaching at the University and who, like us, were waiting for permanent housing.

The luster of living in a hotel (if there was "luster") wore off quickly, and we began looking for alternatives. Through our friendship with Fremont, we learned of a family with the Mennonite Ministries organization, who would be going on home leave for about three months and who would be happy to have someone living in their house while they were gone. After clearing it with the University, we moved into the "Mennonite house," a modest three-bedroom house in a modest but quiet neighborhood. (We also inherited their dog, named Edward...but that's a different story!) We enjoyed having meals in the backyard patio, shaded by a bougainvillea vine and a fig tree. And we got used to seeing cows wandering unattended down our street.

Some weeks later, we were able to move into long-term housing in a development known as The Village. The house was a rambling, but comfortable masonry structure with three bedrooms and ample kitchen, dining, and living space. There was a breezeway connecting the sleeping and the living areas. Outside, there were brave remnants of a garden (yard) and a lawn, most of which had long since been defeated by drought. (We saved our wastewater and poured it around the few plantings that we nursed in the hope they would survive.) The kids, who had meanwhile been admitted into English Medium schools, biked across town to their schools. Years before, at independence, city planners had laid out generous "greenways" across the city for walking and biking, steering pedestrians and bikers clear of motor traffic. However, due to the ongoing drought and lack of maintenance, the greenways were taken over by thorn bushes with sandy footpaths threading between them. Try as they might to avoid them, bike riders who followed the footpaths had a better than average chance of picking up thorns—razor-sharp, some of them were two inches long—in their tires. We became adept at an almost daily routine of repairing punctured bike tires until we discovered that there was such a thing as puncture-proof tires—not perfect, but they helped.

Settling into something of a daily routine, we found that life in Gaborone could, in some ways, be imagined as similar to life in the

US. I went to work—though earlier than I was used to in Pennsyl-vania—the kids went to school and MaDonna busied herself with a variety of activities both in an out of the home. But there were differ-ences, of course. For one thing, the day began early, while it was still relatively cool (the kids' school day began at 7:00 AM) and everyone went home from work or school for an extended lunch break, return-ing to work or school in mid-afternoon where one might stay until early evening. MaDonna found that going to the market could be a daily chore, often going from one small shop to another for specific items. (The first supermarket arrived in Gaborone after we'd been liv-ing there for a few years.) We came to expect—and reluctantly ac-cept—that there were always long lines at the post office and the bank. Sometimes, if it happened to be tea time, we might need to wait at the window while the clerk drank tea and ate a biscuit (cook-ies or a scone).

In spite of being steeped in my Amish (and middle-class Amer-ican) do-it-yourself culture, we discovered that hiring locals to do house and yard work was seen by the potential workers as a kind of obligation of us expatriates—we, they believed, had money and they, with limited opportunities for earning, didn't. It was a point made to us early on by a young man who had come to our door looking for work; I had just told him that we wouldn't be hiring anyone, that we'd do the work ourselves. He responded angrily. It was unfair, he said in his broken English, that I would not hire him. I was just being selfish, keeping my money for myself. That, to us, was a novel way of looking at it, but we had to admit it made sense from his point of view. But his point was taken, and we hired a gardener and household help who stayed with us during most of our years in Gaborone. Most middle-class houses had a small two-room building in their backyard dubbed "servant's quarters" (one room for the gardener, and one for the house worker). Sometimes the workers lived more or less perma-nently in the quarters, but more commonly they would have a home and family in another village or town and go there on weekends, just staying in the "quarters" on the days they were working. We made a point of getting to know our "helpers" and their families, but the arrangement still felt awkward to many of us from Europe and North America. The locals, on the other hand, simply saw it as an important and acceptable means of employment. (Middle-class Africans also hired such help, but the workers typically preferred working for Americans or Europeans as they were said to pay better.)

Becoming part of the community and participating in community events became an important part of our lives in Gaborone. Our family was active members of an expertly conducted community choir that, over the years, performed significant choral works, often accompanied by a small orchestra. Our youngest son, Daryl, who would become a professional baritone as an adult, made his "debut" as a ten-year-old boy soprano in a performance of Mendelsohn's Elijah. For a couple of seasons, I sang next to the Foreign Minister of Botswana in the tenor section of the choir.

In spite of our backgrounds, to the contrary, we found affinity with the liturgical, high-church traditions of the Anglican and UCCSA (United Church of Christ of South Africa) cathedrals. The UCCSA congregation, meeting in a contemporary structure—with remarkably uncomfortable pews—near the downtown mall, held English services on Sunday evenings, and we often attended. I occasionally preached the evening sermon there. An informal, interdenominational reading and discussion group was a regular feature of our Sunday morning routine for some years.

Game parks and game viewing are, of course, a notable and not-to-be-missed part of the expatriate experience[5] in Botswana and neighboring countries. The Kalahari Desert (technically a "semidesert") covered much of the central, western, and southern parts of Botswana, and large swaths of the country have been set aside as game reserves. We made numerous trips into some of the nearby ones with our four-wheel-drive vehicle—an elderly Land Rover with a propensity for refusing to start at inconvenient times. (We were never actually stranded, but came close a time or two; once when we had (inadvisedly!) traveled as a lone vehicle to a remote camp in one of the parks, miles from any other humans.[6] A can of compressed-air starting fluid aimed into the engine's air intake made the difference!) There is something clearly spellbinding—if that's the right word—about rounding a curve and coming face-to-face with a bull elephant in the road, or coming upon a pride of lions (observed from the safety of the vehicle, of course) resting in the shade after a recent kill—not to mention herds of zebra, giraffes, buffaloes, gazelles and more in their natural habitat.

Camping in the remote Kalahari, sometimes with friends, sometimes as a family, was an experience to be remembered. Early mornings were fresh and often dew-drenched; a great time to go out looking for animals. Returning to camp during the heat of the day, one could rest or perhaps read before venturing out again in the cooler afternoon and evening. Despite the daytime heat, nights in the Central Kalahari could be cold—sometimes cold enough to freeze the water in our containers—making a campfire after dark especially pleasant. The Kalahari night sky became unbelievably brilliant after the campfire burned down to embers and lanterns had been extinguished. We could lean back or stretch out on a blanket and marvel: it was hard even to imagine that there could be so many stars—and so close! One wanted to reach up and touch them. Some insisted that in the stillness of the desert night, they could hear the stars hissing and crackling with electric energy.

Neighboring countries offered their own versions of wildness and sights not to be missed. There was the time, for example, that we celebrated Christmas in a grass hut, overlooking Swaziland's spectacular mountains. (Some called them "The Switzerland of Africa.") Another time we made the hours-long, mile-after-mile-after mile drive through desert dust and towering sand dunes from Windhoek, Namibia's capital, to…practically without warning…discover that we had landed in the small, fully German, coastal town of Swakopmund[7] complete with street and shop signs in German and shop owners who greeted you in German.

There was the shock and awe of Victoria Falls, with its mile-wide wall of water falling over a 300-foot precipice, sending up drenching waves of spray and mist. (Not for nothing did the indigenous Zimbabweans call it "The Smoke That Thunders.") Zimbabwe's Hwange National Park was where a park attendant would arrive at your chalet at dinner time to spread a white tablecloth over your table and place the china and silverware for dinner. After the meal, he would reappear to gather up the dirty dishes and the soiled tablecloth for washing. (For a price, one could have had a meal prepared and served as well, with your choice of wild meat.) Then, of course, there was the unparalleled game viewing from a mokoro (an indigenous dugout canoe) in Botswana's famed Okavango Delta. Fed by seasonal rainfall from the mountains of Angola, the Okavango was internationally known as one of Africa's must-see spots. Seated only inches above the crystal-clear water, with a local guide poling from the rear, one had a game viewing experience of a lifetime: multicolored birds, hippos, crocodiles, elephants, zebras, giraffes, and antelopes who barely noticed us gliding silently among them.

It was while we were on vacation in Zimbabwe that I first began growing a beard. I still wear one, some 40 years later. The Amish "ordnung" of course, requires Amish men to wear a beard—sans mustache—when they are about to get married. Not having married "Amish," of course, I had not grown a beard at the time. I don't really know why I chose to do so some 20 years later. Perhaps it was only because it was easier not to shave while staying in a chalet where there was no electricity or running water. Or, maybe it represented something deeper—a kind of latent and late identification with my Amish upbringing? Or did I just like it that way? I really don't know. But I remember that, on my first trip home afterwards, my mother was not very pleased. (She especially disliked the mustache, which the Amish don't allow.) Having been raised in a bearded tradition, she seemed to feel that it was inappropriate for me, who was no longer Amish, to be wearing one. The subject never came up again, but the conversation led to some personal reflection about the nature of self-identity.

But the present, of course, is always shaped by the past. In the latter part of the 19th century, a group of powerful Tswana chiefs, feeling threatened by the Union of South Africa (now the Republic of South Africa) to the south and German Southwest Africa (now Namibia) to the west, petitioned Britain to establish what would become the Protectorate of Bechuanaland. The British complied—reluctantly—dividing the territory into tribal reserves, each under the rule of a hereditary chieftain to whom Britain gave considerable power.

The man who would become the first president of independent Botswana was in the lineage of one such chieftain. Born in 1921 into the royal line of a large and influential tribe, Seretse Khama had been educated in South Africa and England and was studying law at Oxford when he met and then married Ruth Williams, a clerk with Lloyds of London in 1948. A year later, the Union of South Africa passed a law making inter-racial marriage a crime, and the British government, wanting to appease South Africa, responded by banning Khama and his English wife from returning home to Bechuanaland. It was a controversial decision, both in Britain—where some of the English were outraged that an African royal should be treated that way—and in the Protectorate where some tribal leaders (especially Seretse's uncle) were angered because he had not chosen a wife from the tribe. But the ban stood until, in 1956, Khama renounced his right to the tribal throne and the couple was allowed to return home as private citizens.

After his return home, Khama entered politics, forming the Bechuanaland Democratic Party (BDP), and was later easily elected as Prime Minister of the Protectorate. On September 30, 1966, in a process outlined in its new constitution, Seretse Khama was elected as the country's first president. Ten days before Botswana's formal independence, Queen Elizabeth II named him Knight Commander of the Empire (KBE), giving him the title by which he then became known: Sir Seretse Khama.

At the time of independence, Botswana was among the poorest countries in the world. There were fewer than 10 miles of paved roads in the country, only 22 university graduates, and only 100 secondary school graduates. A year after independence, the discovery of extraordinarily rich deposits of diamonds at Orapa, a remote region of the Central Kalahari, would prove to be an economic game-changer. The deposit was said to be the largest in the world.

National policy under Khama's leadership was vigorously progressive and, at the same time, pragmatic, building an export-based economy around beef, copper, and diamonds while also setting up strong measures against corruption. He promoted non-racist policies and practices—a stark contrast to the racial turmoil and war in neighboring states. By the 1970s, Botswana had a budget surplus, which Khama invested in roads, health care, and education at all levels—a project I was to become involved in during my time in the country. Between 1960 and 1980, Botswana was said to have had the fastest-growing economy in the world. Seretse Khama was also a skilled diplomat. Shortly before his death, Khama played a major role in bringing the Rhodesian civil war to an end, resulting in the creation of independent Zimbabwe.

Unlike Botswana, the path to independence for neighboring Zimbabwe was bloody and violent. The so-called Bush War continued even after many of the world's leaders formally recognized the former Rhodesia as independent Zimbabwe in 1980. It was a complicated and drawn-out war with shifting alliances that ultimately pitted then-prime minister Ian Smith's white-ruled Rhodesia against freedom fighters that would eventually bring Robert Mugabe to power. Tens of thousands died, and many more were injured. (When we first visited Zimbabwe on holiday in 1982, there were still parts of the country that were considered no-go zones. I remember the shock of coming upon skeletons of bombed-out buildings beside the road. What had been a more or less abstract account in the news became viscerally real.

Meanwhile, to the south, the armed struggle between the white, apartheid government of South Africa and the ANC (African National Congress) for majority rule was ongoing and also bloody. On one occasion, it would come very close to home—literally. It was in June of our first year in Botswana that we were awakened in the wee hours of the morning by explosions, gunfire, and shouting in a backyard not far from our own. The commotion continued for some time while we hunkered down with no idea of what was going on. It wasn't until morning that reports began filtering out that multiple units of the South African Defense Force had crossed into Botswana and attacked targets in Gaborone, where they believed members of the ANC were living or being sheltered. Twelve people were killed that night, and six were wounded. The explosions and gunfire near us destroyed a servant's quarters in the backyard of a neighbor and killed two people who were living there. Though it was always hard to determine the difference between rumor and fact, it was generally believed that the people killed near us had no connection to the ANC or the armed struggle.

There is no single explanation, it seems, for how it was that Botswana should stand out from its neighbors, even in its early days as a British protectorate, as an example of interracial harmony. Perhaps it could be traced to Britain's apparent lack of interest in colonizing a protectorate, which may have had something to do with the pre-independence perception that Botswana had few natural resources worth exploiting. Perhaps it had something to do with a self-described sense among the majority of Tswana people of being weaker than their more aggressive neighbors, both indigenous and colonial, and opting instead to pursue peaceful coexistence. Perhaps the mixed marriage of the country's first president provided a further example that still sets a kind of standard of racial harmony for the country.

Despite its poverty at independence, Botswana began raising funds almost immediately to establish a national university. The campaign was spearheaded by the president, who dubbed the appeal *motho le motho kgomo* (One Man, One Beast). The people of Botswana—collectively "Batswana"—joined international funding sources, making contributions of cash, cattle, grain, and even eggs, to make the national university a reality. The University of Botswana was formally founded in 1982 (making it only two years old when we arrived in 1984), though it had been offering limited courses as a partner in the predecessor institutions, the University of Botswana and Swaziland (UBS) and the still earlier University of Botswana, Lesotho and Swaziland (UBLS[8]).

The morning after our arrival in the country, I reported to the Registrar's office in the University's administration building for directions. One of the newer buildings on campus, the administration building was a modest, two-story structure of gray-plastered masonry with a blue metal roof. It was connected to other campus buildings by a walkway that was partially shaded by bougainvillea vines. The registrar's office to which I had been directed was on the second floor. I was greeted by the registrar's very efficient assistant, Mrs. Botlhole, who sent me along to the office of Professor Othala, the Dean of Education, where I was again greeted and sent along to the office of the Chair of Educational Psychology, Gholam Kibria, in whose department I would be teaching. Gholam was slight and soft-spoken; a citizen of Bangladesh. It was he who had written the job description to which I had responded months earlier and who had made the decision, in consultation with the dean, to send the teaching contract to me. He greeted me warmly, offered a summary of the department, and outlined my teaching responsibilities, but told me that, sadly, there was no vacant office to which I could be assigned. He hoped one would become available "soon."

My office assignment, when it came through a few weeks later, was to a "caravan," a kind of mobile unit that could house up to four faculty offices. (The caravans were supposed to be temporary, but they weren't really. They were still being used when I left 7 years later.) The units were anything but air-tight, and dust from the nearby Kalahari easily made its way inside. Not to mention insects (both flying and crawling). Lizards lived there too, and played on the ceiling, and I actually became rather fond of them. On one occasion, there was a snake, which prompted a panic among my office neighbors. (I was told afterward the snake was a dangerous one.) The top of my desk, the typewriter (no computers back then), books on the shelf, and even the contents of my desk drawers took on a kind of permanent grittiness from sand carried by the nearly constant wind from the not-too-distant Kalahari. (I was later moved to a new, modern building and a much nicer office directly across from the dean. The building was funded by American—USAID monies.)

Morning "tea" was, we discovered, a deeply entrenched practice in Botswana, and the University was no exception. There was a gathering room designated as the Faculty Tea Room, and each day at mid-morning, staff would bring large kettles of tea and a variety of what the British called biscuits (we would have called them cookies) for a tea break. Many of the faculty would drop whatever they were doing at Tea Time and hike across campus for tea. There was no seating and faculty would come and go as they chose, but it was a time for connecting, for small talk, for socializing, and even, sometimes, serious discussion. Though at first it felt a little strange and like a time waster, I came to enjoy it as a daily ritual and, like most of the faculty, felt a bit cheated when, for some reason or other, there was no tea or I couldn't go.

At the time of UB's founding, there were hardly any Batswana (the collective term for citizens of Botswana) with advanced degrees, so during its formative years, the University relied almost entirely on expatriate faculty. A goodly number were British—thanks to

Botswana's historical ties to Britain—but there were also significant numbers from Canada, the Netherlands, Scandinavia, India, and America, as well as other African countries—even a few that had been educated in Russia. Some of the faculty were sponsored through development projects of their government. The mixture offered a wonderful smorgasbord of nationalities and cultures. It also meant that there were nearly as many theories about how education should be conducted as there were nationalities represented—leading, sometimes, to spirited discussion or, just as often, under-the-breath mutterings.

In the Faculty of Education (equivalent to a school in American parlance), for example, it was clear—though rarely voiced in public—that there was disagreement on how to use textbooks (the Brits used them regularly, the Russians almost exclusively and the Americans tended to use them as supplements), how much lecturing was too much, and how often (or whether) one should give quizzes (Americans were thought generally to give too many quizzes. Some argued that quizzes were unfair and that grades should be based on a final comprehensive exam for which the students could properly prepare, and that "really measured what students had learned.") In the end, most solutions took on a British flavor. That was, after all, the tradition on which the University had been founded and where many of the faculty had been educated, although the Scandinavians and the Dutch were considered level-headed arbiters. (Some thought American courses lacked rigor and that American professors were "soft." Multiple-choice test questions were a kind of American joke.) Notwithstanding the differences, however, there was remarkable respect and collegiality among the faculty.

Though Botswana had done much to expand access to primary and secondary education, resources and seats in schools at all levels were still limited. Admission to junior secondary school (comparable to an American junior high) was only for those who scored at the top of their "Standard Seven leaving exams."[9] (roughly equivalent to American 7th grade, the final year of primary school). Similarly, admission to secondary school (high school) was restricted to those scoring at the top of their Junior Secondary leaving exams. By the same token, admission to the University was based on scores on the Secondary School Leaving exam. The students in our university classes, then, had all come through a strict selection process and were, supposedly, the best of the best—almost all were, indeed, highly motivated and had at least learned how to do well on exams—asking for creative or independent thought was sometimes another matter. But they were a joy to teach, though I was sometimes reminded of how easily words used in different contexts could carry unexpected meanings. It took me a while, for example, to understand that when students told me that they had spent all night "revising," they were not rewriting the syllabus, but were in fact studying it (their notes, of course). I still remember the sudden, uneasy silence when I made a passing comment about someone being "late" (to a meeting). A few students explained to me afterward that, as they understood the word, I had just announced that person's death.

On a different note, I remember my bafflement when, one day, a couple of students seemed to be distracted by something outside and left the room. Other students noticed them and soon followed until the classroom was nearly empty. This sort of behavior was highly unusual since the students were usually very well-behaved and polite. When I asked what was going on I got the explanation: the first students had seen a swarm of flying termites from the window (termites emerge from the ground and swarm only after a rain and are considered a delicacy—with a sort of nutty flavor I was told). Dedicated though they were, my students couldn't resist the temptation for a special treat that might fly away at any time!

Sometimes, students stayed after class and talked about their families and life in their hometown or village, as well as their own hopes and dreams. For some, living in a student hostel (dorm) was their first experience with electric lights and running water. Sometimes they remarked on the lifestyle differences between living in a remote village in the back of the Kalahari and living in the city. While most spoke warmly about their homes and families, it was also quite clear that many saw their university degrees as passports, offering a pathway into middle- or upper-class living and to well-paying jobs. But sometimes, not unlike my students years ago in northwestern Ontario, a kind of ambivalent dichotomy emerged in which they struggled to align the traditional culture, rooted as it was in the village and kinship ties, with modernity and the western worldview represented by the city and the University. Life in the city, in the villages, and in the towns was a starkly different world. By embracing the worlds of the city, they had, in effect, chosen to be exiled from their homes of origin. But some also seemed uncertain of their place in the foreign world of modernity. Trying to align those worlds could be complicated and disorienting.

But the students were representatives of a gracious people: generous, ready to share with others and offer hospitality to strangers. They were heirs to a long tribal tradition of hearing and respecting every voice and resolving issues by discussion, best exemplified in the "village kgotla:" a space in the center of the village where any person could request a hearing by the village elders, who would listen to both sides and then make a judgment.

My department chair, Gholam, and I learned to know each other well. We worked together on several projects, including some collaborative research on special education needs in the country's primary schools. I developed a deep respect for what he represented. He was Muslim, the father of three young children, one of whom was developmentally disabled. He told me harrowing stories of being caught in the middle of the Indo-Pakistan conflict just over a decade earlier[10] and having to flee with his wife and small daughters in the dark of night. He and his wife somehow managed to carry their small children and a few personal belongings over a mountain trail made slippery by rain. It was a story of suffering and personal faith in a world about which, I was ashamed to admit, I had known next to nothing. I gained a deep appreciation for his worldview, his sacrifices to care for his family, and his commitment to his faith.

A few months before the end of my second year at UB, I was invited to renew my contract for a second two-year term. That wasn't how we had planned it, but things were going well at the University, our children were happy in their schools and MaDonna, though legally unable to work for pay since she didn't have a work permit, had found ways to connect with other women, both African and western and was doing volunteer work in a couple of different places. In the end, the decision to renew my contract for two more years was not a difficult one. After I'd signed the contract, we began planning for a month of home leave.

During my first year at UB, I was asked to become chair of the faculty's graduate studies committee, a position with considerable power over the master's degree programs (there were, at the time, no doctoral programs). After a faculty-wide meeting that I had convened and just a week or so after I'd signed the contract with UB for a second term, I was approached by Max, the leader of an Ohio University team (based at UB and funded by USAID) for improving primary education in Botswana. The Ohio project, known as the Primary Education Improvement Project or PEIP, was wrapping up the first 5-year phase of a successful project and was in the process of submitting plans for a second five-year phase. One of the key features, among others, of the new phase was developing and implementing a master's degree program specifically for faculty in the teacher training colleges, many of whom only held bachelor's degrees (a few of the colleges had been established by the first phase of PEIP). Max asked whether I would consider joining their team for the project's second phase. I would become a member of the Ohio University faculty, seconded to UB—a dual appointment. I would serve as a "Specialist in Research and Design," responsible for conducting research and for developing and implementing the new master's degree.

I would continue to carry faculty rank at UB, continue serving as the chair of UB's master's degree committee, and teach courses in the Faculty of Education as time permitted.

The project was attractive, and though I asked for time to think it over and discuss it with the family, this too was not a hard decision—subject, of course, to UB's willingness to release me from the contract I had just signed. Accepting the offer would mean we were making a commitment to stay in Botswana for at least five more years. But we had, by that time, adjusted to Botswana and felt good about staying, though there were still times when we felt like strangers in the land. An added perk of the Ohio/USAID contract was that, in addition to home leave every two years, our family would, in the in-between years, be entitled to a travel allowance for R&R (Rest and Recuperation) equivalent to air fare from Gaborone to New York or Rome. We could use the allowance for travel anywhere so long as we stayed within those overall limits. It was a generous allowance which, when combined with travel to and from the States on home leave every two years, made it possible for our family to travel broadly. By the time we left Botswana, we had visited countries on each of the world's seven continents, except Antarctica. (I was additionally able to make several international trips to conferences where I presented research papers—but not in Antarctica.)

Becoming a member of the Ohio team also meant traveling within Botswana, collecting research data, making presentations, and conducting workshops. During this time, I also served as an "external examiner"[11] for the University of Zimbabwe in Harare and for several of Zimbabwe's outlying Teacher Training Colleges, making several trips to Zimbabwe on those assignments. As I came to know them, my respect and admiration for the people of Southern Africa deepened. One could only be impressed by their ways of thinking about the world, by their strong sense of community and unfailing hospitality, their readiness to share scarce resources, and their willingness, sometimes, to just persevere in spite of what seemed like an infinite spiral of political and economic chaos.

As we moved into the fifth and final year of the Ohio project, our family was faced with the What Next? Question: Would I stay on at UB as a long-term expatriate professor (I had been reviewed and promoted twice by UB and could have stayed on as a resident expatriate member of the UB faculty had I chosen to), or would we return to the States at the end of the project? It was commonly accepted among academics from America or abroad that while it was good to have international experience on one's vitae, it was also possible to stay abroad too long—the assumption being, rightly or wrongly, that the longer one stayed abroad, the more one would have begun losing touch with the cutting edge of one's field. The longer one stayed abroad, the more difficult it would be to get plugged back into one's home system. So a decision to extend our stay in Botswana still longer could mean that I would, perhaps of necessity, finish my career there. I knew colleagues who had made that decision and seemed happy with it.

But there were also family considerations. Our oldest son, Rodney, had finished his secondary schooling in Botswana a few years earlier, earning what, in the British system, is known as an A Level certificate—roughly equivalent to the first year of college in the American system—and, after exploring college options, had settled on Reed College in Portland, Oregon. He began his studies there while we were still living in Botswana. We had been on home leave in the States the summer before he began his freshman year and had been able to visit the college before he made his final decision, but saying good-bye to him at the airport was hard.

We had already planned that he would come to Botswana for the summer between his freshman and sophomore years, but we also experimented with developing a kind of cobbled-together communication channel that would be faster than the weeks it took letters to make their way back and forth. Working with a friend in Botswana who ran a computer business, we eventually established a kind of email system by which we could exchange messages once a week or so using private computer bulletin boards on each end and tying into a link for transferring data between a university in South Africa and one in Oregon.[12] But regardless, having an 18-year-old son on the other side of the world was a heavy lift.

Our daughter, Karla, would be finishing her secondary school studies at the end of my term with Ohio—also having completed A-Levels—and was expecting to attend a still-to-be-determined college somewhere in the States the following fall. Our third child, Daryl, was only a year behind. These all figured prominently in the conclusion we eventually reached that the time had come to move back to the States.

But it was not an easy decision. World news made its way to Botswana, and Burdick and Lederer's 1958 book *The Ugly American* still resonated with many. There were times we would have preferred not to be identified as Americans. We felt good, of course, about some of what America did and represented abroad and at home—the USAID/Ohio project with which I was affiliated being a case in point. But there were many times when our country of origin didn't make us proud. I remember cringing when, standing next to an English friend at the American Ambassador's Fourth of July picnic, the Ambassador declaimed at some length his version of why America was "the greatest country on earth for doing good." My English friend just looked at me and rolled his eyes. Neither of us needed to say more. Our children would tell us later that they tried not to be identified as Americans; there was too much baggage associated with being American, they said.

Our experience of church and of the nature of religious practice had also taken on a different perspective. Perhaps it was in some way a perspective inherited from my Amish roots (which is, in its own way, liturgical—certainly ritualistic), but after a less-than-happy experience with Southern Baptists, we found meaningful congruence with the more liturgical traditions such as Anglican and United Church of Christ South Africa. We also came to appreciate non-Christian ones, as having their own validity; views that would have been seen with much suspicion or rejected out of hand by the Amish and Mennonites of our heritage. While still valuing aspects of my inherited traditions, my identity with them was no longer as clear nor as strong as it had once been. Despite the tendency of those traditions, and most others for that matter, to frame and value their experience of faith and religious practice in their own inherited terms, I came to understand that valid religious traditions and experiences were much larger and broader than those I had inherited.

Living on the other side of the globe from the familiarity of the people and cultures of our origins changed our frames of reference. The taken-for-granted criteria we had formerly used to classify others—naming their beliefs or cultural practices as strange or different—no longer worked. Now it was our own ways of seeing and of being in the world that came under scrutiny. We had to learn a new language: a language of cultures that was just as real as a language of words and sentences. It was a "language" that forced us to create new categories and taught us to think of others in new ways. Perhaps we were the "different" or "strange" ones and not the other way around. Almost imperceptibly, we had begun discovering new freedoms; freedom to ask hard questions, freedom to name things as we saw them. We had discovered worlds for which our familiar categories no longer worked. We would need to figure out whether, and if so, how, to be "in" them even if, for any number of reasons, we couldn't be "of" them.

Maybe we had been abroad too long, but America began to seem increasingly distant and foreign, even unattractive. Maybe we had become the adult versions of third culture kids; kids living abroad with their families who could no longer identify with their home country, but who couldn't fully belong to the country in which they are living either. Our "betweenness" wasn't defined by the passports we carried; it had more to do with the changes in the cultural languages we now spoke and had begun to understand. We had, figuratively speaking, turned in our birthright[14] citizenship but were not citizens in any other way either.

It was with mixed feelings, then, that we made the decision to return to the States in the late summer of 1991. USAID would ship our belongings from Botswana to our designated home in the US. Seven years earlier, our family had boarded a plane at Portland's International Airport with five bags and five small trunks plus what we could carry. Now our things would come to us in the hold of a seagoing freighter. But we were bringing back so much more than the contents of a shipping container. Our sense of ourselves, of the world, and of our place in it had been fundamentally altered. We were no longer the same people who had boarded a United Airlines flight to Africa seven years before.

++++++

[1] Decades later urban sprawl, shopping centers and bypass highways have made the city unrecognizable to those of us who knew it in the 1980s.

[2] We got considerable amusement from the directional sign newly erected along the highway when the new airport opened. Drivers were directed, according to the sign, to the "Sir Seretse Khama International Airport."

[3] No pun intended, but this is true both literally and figuratively. The average height is about 5 feet. But they also left little trace of their presence on the land.

[4] A special kind of grass stayed green year-round, thanks to a built-in sprinkler system that came on every morning.

[5] Less so, it seemed, for those who had grown up in the region. Other than official park rangers or guides (or in the scattered village), it was unusual to see Africans in game parks. Perhaps having

grown up among the animals, so to speak, made them less interesting?

[6] An important rule about traveling into the interior of the Kalahari was that there should always be at least two vehicles traveling together so that in case of a breakdown, the second vehicle could serve as a backup. We were foolhardy but fortunate in that ignoring the rule didn't, in this case, end in disaster!

[7] Swakopmund had been our destination of course, so we did expect to get there. But finding a "real German town" on the edge of the desert in Africa was an interesting shock. A 1976 article in the New York times described Swakopmund as "more German than Germany." (Kamm, H., NYT, October 39, 1976), We learned later of the town's darker role before and during both World Wars.

[8] Some of the buildings on campus, when I arrived, had been constructed under the auspices of these earlier institutions.

[9] At the end of each level of schooling (primary, junior secondary, secondary, etc.), students sat for a comprehensive exam. Students' names and their scores were posted on public bulletin boards. These were the so-called "Cambridge Examinations." The exams came from England and were sent back to England for grading, accounting for substantial wait time in order to get results.

[10] This was the Indo-Pakistan War of 1971 that created millions of refugees and resulted in the creation of Bangladesh.

[11] In keeping with a British tradition in higher education, universities and colleges in Southern Africa implemented an External Examiner system whereby an unaffiliated person reviews student exams given by a college or university to ensure the accuracy of grading.

[12] The internet and email, as we now know it, did not yet exist in the late 1980s. (We composed and uploaded messages on private (electronic) bulletin boards (BBS) in Gaborone and Portland. From our BBS in Gaborone, we uploaded the messages to the University of Witwatersrand in South Africa, who bundled our little message

with a massive data exchange with Portland State University. The local BBS in Portland was downloaded, and Rodney could dial in and download his email.

[13] During a sabbatical in Germany, I worshipped at the Catholic cathedral. Despite the language barriers, something happened there that was both broader and deeper than what I experienced in the traditions of my origins.

[14] Thank you, Jonathan Larsen.

Part IV: Recursions

We shall not cease from exploration
And the end of all our exploring
Will be to arrive where we started
And know the place for the first time.
- T.S. Eliot from *Little Gidding*

In Homer's epic myth of Odysseus, the hero comes full circle as he turns toward home after years of adventure, conquest and hardship abroad. When he finally arrives, he finds that things are not as they used to be; his young son is grown, his wife is besieged by would-be suitors and friends who were once young are now old. Then, directed by a blind seer, he finds he must go on one more journey. He is to carry a "well cut oar" into the hinterland where no one has ever heard of the sea, much less the strange object he is carrying. He is to plant the oar upside down at a cross-road where "...its roots will go down and green shoots with leaves will spring out and fruit will come forth." When citizens of that land ask about the strange tree, he is to tell them of the sea and of the worlds beyond, worlds of which they know nothing. He is to tell of struggle and conquest and wisdom acquired. He will find the meaning of his journey in the in the telling of it to those who ask. And leaving us to ponder what the wisdom of old age can contribute by such telling.

{ eight }

On Being Swiss Among Russians

Fresno, California, was in the grip of a heat wave when we landed there in mid-August. Karla and Daryl were with us, and Rodney was finishing up a summer internship abroad before returning to his fourth year of college in Portland. The Vice President for Academics at Fresno Pacific College met us at the airport and temporarily installed us in an unoccupied suite in one of the college dorms. Most of our things were somewhere on the Pacific Ocean or somewhere on an interstate highway in a westbound truck. It was a strange feeling of displacement—of somehow being nowhere in the middle of somewhere.

It was in the fall of the previous year, while we were still in Botswana, that I came across a notice in a higher education periodical, inviting applications for the position of dean of graduate studies at Fresno Pacific College in Fresno, California. I recognized the name, but knew little about Fresno or Fresno Pacific College—only that both were in California, and I thought the college had been founded by the Mennonite Brethren Church (both of which turned out to be correct). I was actively in the job market by then and sent a letter of inquiry to the college. It wasn't long before I received a reply from the Vice President for Academics inviting me to apply. He went on to say that he thought I might be a good fit for the position, though he couldn't have had much to go on at that time. I formalized the application and was subsequently invited to an on-campus interview. We agreed that I could visit the campus and conduct the interview during our family's upcoming holiday break over Christmas.

Home leave, when it came, was eventful. In addition to the interview at Fresno Pacific, I interviewed for a faculty position at an Ohio university. I had a telephone interview for a very different position as a specialist with a large international firm in Chicago that published tests for schools and universities. Then there were college visits with Karla. She had been narrowing her college choices, and the two of us flew to visit colleges from my parents' home in Virginia before I flew on to Fresno. MaDonna and Daryl would fly, meanwhile, from Virginia to her parents' home in Oregon, where I would join them after the interview at Fresno Pacific. Karla would fly directly to Oregon from one of her campus visits. We'd meet Rodney in Oregon, where he was attending Reed College in Portland.

The interview process at Fresno Pacific at that time included something called a "pilgrimage." This was a truncated life story presented at an open meeting of the faculty, which, in theory at least, provided the faculty with a window into the candidate and offered them the opportunity to discern how well the candidate's experience and worldview might align with the college ethos. I tried to be both diplomatic and honest, but probably didn't use some of the language expected by some. Nevertheless, the day after the interview, I received a phone call from the VPAA offering me the position. I was pleased—I did need a job, after all—but was hesitant to accept until I had heard from the other places where I had interviewed and could weigh the options. I was also ambivalent about how well I might fit into the institutional culture at Fresno Pacific. I asked for a couple of days to consider.

While I was hesitating, I received a personal—and certainly unofficial—letter from one of the senior faculty at Fresno Pacific, who wrote to say that he had sensed I may have had some discomfort with some of the conservative religious language I had heard on campus. He wanted me to know, he wrote, that "...there is more to us than that." It was a thoughtful and welcome gesture and probably helped me reach the decision, shortly thereafter, to accept the position. The salary was the highest among the options, and I was given the impression that I would have considerable freedom to develop the graduate programs as I saw fit.

Later, after getting to know the campus better, I would discover a simmering, though low-level and largely unspoken, division between a more progressive wing of faculty (including the one who had written to me) and the college president, who, along with the Board of Trustees, was inclined toward a more strict "evangelicalism" and wanted to move the college in that direction. Regardless, it felt good, during my last months in Botswana, to know that I had a job waiting for me.

Within a few days of arriving in Fresno, we rented an unfurnished house in North Fresno and, after an extended stop at a nearby department store, became the proud owners of some basic cookware, packages of paper plates and plastic cutlery, sleeping bags, folding lawn chairs—and a good stereo set that was on sale. The college connected us with an excellent realtor, and within a few weeks, we settled on a place that was within walking distance of the college. Our mortgage application was approved, and before we knew it, we had taken ownership of a modest piece of California real estate. (The actual owner, of course, was the bank.)

It didn't take long, though, for reverse culture shock to set in—the shock of discovering that returning to one's culture of origin could be even more disorienting than leaving it. Some of the shock came from experiencing new and strange things and then feeling stupid because we hadn't known about them. We were impressed, for example, by the black box, about the size of a large shoe box, that rested on the seat of the realtor's car as he took us from place to place. He could pull up to a house and, using a handset on top of the box, call the owner to say that they were parked on the street outside their house and could they come in? Then there was the microwave oven in our new kitchen, and we destroyed several perfectly good pieces of Tupperware before we figured out the finer points of microwaving. Check-out clerks in the supermarket no longer keyed numbers into a cash register; instead, they slid items across a light that activated a screen showing the item's name and price. We were embarrassed by the strange looks of passersby as they watched us trying to figure out how to manage parking meters.

We had to unlearn the spelling of words according to the "Queen's English" and relearn the American versions; words such as *labor* instead of *labour* or *color* instead of *colour.* There was also a vocabulary we had adopted in Gaborone that had to be unlearned: cars once again had a trunk instead of a boot, and the engine compartment was again protected by a hood instead of a bonnet. Instead of having petrol pumped into our car, we had to operate the pumps ourselves in order to fill the tank with something called "gas"—of all things! We had to learn to drive on the right-hand side of the road again (not so bad, really, but making left-hand turns could be tricky), and that a backyard barbecue was no longer a braai.[1] People waiting to be served were once again standing in a line instead of a queue, and an order of French fries was once again accompanied by ketchup instead of vinegar.

Some of the dislocated feelings came from things that had become part of our daily routine in Botswana, and we now realized how much we missed them. We missed the smell and texture of the freshly baked wheat bread that was delivered, unwrapped, in the open bed of a bakie (a small pickup truck) every afternoon to shops all around town. (We bought ours from a nearby corner market called the *No Mathata Market,* roughly translated as the No-Problem Market. American white bread didn't even deserve a comparison.) We missed the ubiquitous, bright-colored bougainvillea and the jacaranda and syringa trees that burst into bloom in spring, even during the worst of the multi-year drought. Most of all, of course, we missed the people; the people with whom we had shared those spaces and who had been companions on our journey over the last seven years. We had to get used to the blank looks on faces when we—inadvertently at first—made references to African or international matters. Most Americans, it seemed, were not very knowledgeable nor very interested in things outside of their borders, and we learned to steer conversations in other directions. It was clear: we were now in California:[2] the US of A! But for a time, we felt like strangers in what was supposed to be our homeland. Sometimes it seemed we were walking around in a dream; at other times, we seemed to be watching ourselves as though from a distance.

Fresno Pacific College, I would learn, had at first been established as a West Coast sister to a Mennonite Brethren college in Kansas, Tabor College. I knew little about either the college or about the Mennonite Brethren in spite of them being theological relatives within the broad groups of Anabaptists (re-baptizers—for their belief in adult baptism) of which the Amish and Mennonites, among whom I had grown up, could be considered a sub-group. The Anabaptists had suffered severe persecution—imprisonment, confiscation of property, and martyrdom—as early as the 16th century at the hands of the Swiss government and by both the Catholic and the Reformed Church authorities in Switzerland.

As a result, the Swiss Anabaptists (the movement's origins were in Switzerland) began moving northward into what is now Germany, France, and the Netherlands, where they would eventually find a measure of tolerance or migrate onward to places where they could find acceptance. By the 18th and 19th centuries, many Amish and Mennonites of Swiss and German origin had begun emigrating to America, mostly landing in Pennsylvania, from where they would spread westward. The descendants of these Swiss/German immigrants were the Amish (and Mennonites) among whom I had been raised and encultured. This denominational family, varied though they were, considered themselves the root of the Anabaptist movement.

However, some in the group that would later be known as Mennonite Brethren also thought of themselves in this way. They had come to America later and by a different route, but also traced their roots to the Swiss Anabaptists. However, their cultural roots were in the Netherlands (and later in Central and Eastern Europe). Instead of crossing the Atlantic to North America, this group, under pressure in the Netherlands, migrated eastward toward Poland (later Prussia) and then to the southern Russian Empire (now Ukraine). This group came to be known as the "Russian Mennonites." They had surnames like Enns, Wiebe, Toews, Klassen, Braun, Friezen, and Janzen, rather than Swiss-German names such as Yoder, Miller, Gingerich, Hochstetler, and Wenger. The Russian Mennonites spoke "Plautdietsch" (an East Low German dialect that is not understood by the Amish speakers of Pennsylvania Dutch who were of Swiss origin). Some among the Mennonites in Russia had been heavily influenced, theologically, by the Pietists[3] and Moravian Brethren, who had also fled to Eastern Europe to escape persecution in Germanic and French Europe.

The Mennonites from the Netherlands were recognized and welcomed by Prussian nobles as skilled and hard-working farm workers. Over many decades, the Polish Mennonites developed "...a lifestyle of religious tradition and cultural conservatism."[4] This changed in 1772, when the region came under Prussian rule, and it became impossible for the Mennonites to sustain their lifestyle and autonomy. Meanwhile, the Empress of Russia, Catherine "The Great," invited the Mennonites (as well as others) who wanted to leave Prussia to settle in southern Russia (now Ukraine), again welcoming their skill as farmers, builders, and tradespeople. Many of the Prussian Mennonites accepted the invitation, viewing it as a "Godsend," and large numbers migrated there in the late 1700s and early 1800s. Catherine promised them freedom to exercise their faith and exemption from military service. The Mennonites' early years in Russia were challenging, but over time, they prospered, forming self-governing,

German-speaking communities and establishing schools, clinics, and hospitals. As time passed, the elders of the Mennonite church in Russia began to act as civil authorities within the Russian government system.

However, the welcome of the Mennonites in Russia also came to an end as political alliances shifted, and Catherine's promises were either ignored or rescinded. Life in Russia became untenable for the Mennonites. By the latter 19th and early 20th centuries, tens of thousands had migrated to the United States and Canada as well as to Paraguay, Brazil, and Mexico.[5] Some of these immigrants, especially those outside the US, formed German-speaking colonies in the hope of retaining the life they had lived in Russia. But others, including those represented by the founders of Fresno Pacific, by now known as Mennonite Brethren, adapted to the prevailing culture in many ways while still retaining their theological and religious identity. Superficially, at least, they became indistinguishable from mainstream American and Canadian cultures, while retaining their religious distinctives as well as a within-group identity based on kinship ties and a shared history.

The MBs (as they became known in the US and Canada) not only brought with them their pietistic theology and practice, they also brought a deeply embedded culture that was shaped, in part at least, by the marginalization they had experienced at the hands of authorities in both Poland/Prussia and Russia/Ukraine. Living as they had, largely in self-governing communities and, later, under persecution by the authorities, the cultural and social lines, as well as the religious ones, between "us" (the Russian Mennonites including the MBs) and "them"—the non-Mennonites—were sharply drawn. We learned, for example, of iconic foods such as vereniki, borscht, "zwieback" (literally, "twice-baked" bread), and customs such as "faspa"[6] that, simple though they seemed, were cultural markers. When we said that we'd never heard of zwieback or faspa, we immediately became cultural outsiders. We weren't rejected, we were just on the other side of that cultural boundary. Our origins were Swiss; we were not—and couldn't be—"of" the Russians' world. Though Yoders were widespread among Amish and Mennonite communities farther east, the name was uncommon in California, and we got used to being asked "How do you spell that?" after telling someone our name. Although we counted many Russians as close friends, we could never fully be part of their world. They had rich familial and historical networks of acquaintances, friends, and relatives spread across parts of the US and Canada, which meant nothing to us and with which we had no points of connection. We carried a different set of "cultural and familial chromosomes."

Coming to know Mennonites with Russian roots made us more keenly aware of our own inherited Swiss-German culture—born hundreds of years ago but still present in some subtle and some not-so-subtle expressions. We too had an engrained sub-culture that while not always visible or recognized, was still present. We too had inherited a frame of reference by which to see and interpret the world. We had inherited elements of a common culture that made it easy to connect with our own kind and to draw lines between "us" and "them." Our shared surnames made it easy to begin what was sometimes called the "Mennonite Game" of figuring out how one might be related to a new acquaintance. We knew of each others' communities; some of us had gone to the same colleges and many of us had at least a sense of having had Swiss-German ancestors and, often, some sense of how and when they had found their way to the New World. It was easy for those who didn't share that cultural language—a "cultural DNA"--to find themselves on the other side of an invisible boundary line.

Over time, we developed our own identity within the community. We were accepted for who we were: Mennonites with a different set of roots and a different cultural background. Paradoxically, despite the obvious differences, the Mennonite Brethren's deeply ingrained sense of having been "other" only a few generations before was, in some ways, not unlike that of the Amish of my origins[7]—different though they were in modern lifestyle. Both shared stories of being different, of living outside mainstream culture, of persecution, and of border and boundary markers that separated them from others outside their communities. They were, each in their own ways, "in but not of" the surrounding cultures.

I pondered a remark made by a senior member of the Fresno Pacific faculty, who is also a descendant of Russian Mennonites. Over lunch with a handful of faculty colleagues in a small cafe near the University, I had casually remarked—I no longer remember the context—that maybe I was "still sort of Amish" in some ways. "Oh yes," he responded, "You are still Amish. You can't hide it." I'm not sure what he meant by the remark. I don't believe he had ever lived among the Amish, nor had he had any direct experience with them, but I took the comment as affirmation. The comment reminded me that cultural social threads woven into one's life tapestry are not easily hidden. I've since wondered whether he and I were experiencing a "cultural recognition reflex," of some sort, however faint and subtle, stemming from our common histories of having lived behind boundaries that separated "us" from "them." This notion was reinforced by my friendship with one of the college's past presidents.[8] —now long retired. He was a second-generation immigrant from Russia but seemed to have a kind of intuitive understanding of my Amish background, though he had never lived among them and, so far as I knew, had probably not known any Amish personally. Whether and how such "cultural DNA" finds expression, and how it may be transmitted across generations, is not obvious, but one might suspect it to be more real than is often recognized.

This was the cultural and religious narrative that had shaped the vision of Fresno Pacific College's founders.[9] But by the time I arrived, the pragmatics of institutional survival had led to expansion, including the development of several professional graduate programs, mainly in specialties within Education, which, I was to learn, had become a source of some friction among the faculty.

The graduate faculty, for the most part, was not of Mennonite Brethren origin. They were professionals, including linguists, psychologists, historians, and educators, and represented a more pragmatic, "marketplace-oriented" approach. They sometimes felt frustrated by the undergraduate faculty, who, they believed, did not understand the purposes and mission of the graduate programs and were sometimes unwilling to support academic proposals coming from the graduate faculty. For the undergraduate liberal arts faculty, college was about forming a life as much as it was about acquiring knowledge in a major. For the graduate faculty, on the other hand, personal values were subsumed under professional ones. It was a difference that I once characterized as a kind of tension between "monastery and marketplace."[10]

My first meeting with the graduate faculty, before the start of my first semester at Fresno, was memorable. I had learned that they had a reputation for being "grumpy," believing they were not understood and were not being listened to by the other faculty members. I came to that meeting with a large blank pad on an easel. After formalities, we began listing their concerns and ideas for change. We filled multiple pages on the easel pad that afternoon. That session was significant because, I believe, it set a tone and direction for my relationships with the graduate faculty as a group and as individuals. We successfully set the stage for both personal and professional bonding. The occasional, unsolicited notes of appreciation and support from the faculty were, to me, priceless. Ten years later, when I announced to a meeting of the graduate faculty that I was leaving the post, they responded with dismay—but offered their best wishes.

Those years as dean of the Fresno Pacific Graduate School were, especially in hindsight, among the most satisfying of my career. Not only were they satisfying on a professional and personal level, they were also important by easing, incrementally, the journey from

Africa toward this now strange land called America; a place that should have been home but wasn't really.

But California, as we experienced it, was unique **as a** "place" as well as **a** people, and our years there were clearly colored by that sense. Our home was in Fresno, the largest city in the San Joaquin Valley, also known as the Central Valley, but we roamed far and wide within the region. The arid environment, with its sparse grasses, dusty weeds along the roadsides, and stifling midday heat in summer, was unex-pectedly reminiscent of the Africa we had left behind. But the irri-gation canals criss-crossing the valley and the vast acres of irrigated orchards and crop-lands[11] made it clear that this was not Botswana!(The seasons were, of course, reversed; we had left Gaborone in mid-winter and, crossing the equator, arrived in Fresno in mid-summer.) The occasional bougainvillea vines—far fewer than in Africa — the jacaranda and mimosa trees in a few front yards and along the ir-rigation canals all felt familiar. However, it was the foothills a few miles to the east and, just beyond them, the snow-capped Sierra Nevada Mountains, rising to over 12,000 feet, that defined the differ-ences most dramatically. In the other direction, to our west, though not in our line of sight, was the Coastal Range, beyond which was San Francisco and the Bay Area. Between the two mountain ranges lay the Central Valley, extending from Sacramento in the north to Bakersfield, approximately 280 miles to the south. Our home in Fresno was roughly in the middle.

We spent weekends in San Francisco and other places on the west side of the Coastal Range, especially enjoying an area south of San Francisco known as the Central Coast. But we spent more time roaming the Sierra foothills, marveling at the early spring splendor of mile after mile of fruit trees in full blossom and enjoying the just-picked flavors of peaches, oranges, and strawberries. We discovered that by driving only a short distance into the foothills above Fresno, we could find welcome relief from the summer heat as well as from the tule fogs[12] that could settle over the valley for days at a time in winter. At an altitude of just a thousand feet or so, one could emerge into brilliant winter sunshine while looking down on the dark, greasy-looking fog enshrouding the Valley. Our favorite places, though, were still higher in the nearby national parks: Yosemite and the lesser-known Sequoia, which have spectacular peaks, lush alpine meadows, and towering Sequoia trees. We could be at Yosemite's south entrance in less than an hour from our front door, and we took every opportunity to go there. It was especially enjoyable to show off our favorite spots in the parks to family and friends who came to visit, places that the average tourist might not even be aware of. Our lifetime National Park pass card got plenty of use.

We also learned that the weather on the mountains could be fickle. There was, for example, the time one early October that MaDonna and I had arranged to spend a long weekend in a friend's cabin in a small village just outside of the Yosemite entrance. It was hot when we left the city, probably in the upper-90s (Fahrenheit) or higher. We noticed some thunder clouds in the west as we left the city, but thought nothing of them; perhaps we'd have to drive through a shower or two along the way. Rain began falling as we made our way into the foothills. As we began to gain altitude, the raindrops took on a slushy appearance, and as we drove higher still, large, fluffy snowflakes began falling on our windshield. Snow? But this was October!

We slowed down, but kept going, certain that we'd soon be out of it. However, the snow became thicker and began piling up on the road, obscuring the lane markings and the verges, where we knew there were steep drop-offs, often unprotected by a barrier. No one else was on the road, and as the snow began accumulating, we wondered whether we should turn back, but with the drop-offs on one side and the embankment on the other, turning around seemed dangerous and inadvisable. It was getting dark by this time; the road was becoming treacherous, and since the markers that we normally relied on to tell us where we were were no longer visible, we couldn't judge our location. Landmarks that would normally have told us where we were had become invisible in the snow and the dark. Going back to get out of the storm might actually be farther than going on toward our destination. I'm not sure how long we kept driving—slowly—in these conditions; it seemed like hours.

Eventually, we were stopped by flashing warning lights and a barrier across the road. A traffic officer standing nearby informed us that the road ahead was closed; we wouldn't be allowed to proceed any further. We were directed into a roadside parking area next to a nearby lodge where, the officer said, we could "probably" spend the night—in the lobby if not in a room. However, we also learned from him that we had stopped just short of our destination. Our cabin was barely a half-mile downhill. We managed to get our car into the lodge's parking lot, where we had left it, and, dragging our overnight bags, made our way downhill in the direction of the village. It was dark and still snowing, and we were wearing only light summer shoes and light jackets! But wet and cold as we were, we couldn't escape the magic of the moment: snow falling silently out of a dark sky, the lights of the village beginning to twinkle in the distance—the stuff of Christmas cards. Some thirty minutes later, we found our cabin, glad to be in a place that was warm, dry, and safe! The next morning dawned clear, bright, cold, and beautiful: pristine, untracked snow blanketing everything against a gloriously blue sky. More magic. Our plans for the weekend had to change, of course—the road into Yosemite was still closed—but we enjoyed tramping in the snow (with borrowed boots and cold weather gear), reading in front of the wood fire, watching birds coming to the feeders. We drove home the next evening on dry roads. When we got to Fresno, people there said: "Snow? What snow?"

It was an ironic twist that couldn't have been planned: some eleven years after landing in California, we found ourselves on the way to Kansas, the state of my birth and where my parents and grandparents were rooted. The decision to move to Kansas evolved over the space of only a few months and, in another irony, would likely never have happened had it not been for the encouragement and advice of my mentor and then-interim president at Fresno Pacific.

In the previous summer, the president of Fresno Pacific University had resigned, and the presidency was declared open. When the Board of Trustees appointed an interim president, and it became clear that no internal candidate would be considered, the provost, who might have been first in line, also resigned. He, the provost, called me at home the morning before he was to make the announcement public, adding that he expected I would be named his successor shortly. I was honored, but I had mixed feelings; it was a "hot seat" position, and I was content in my role as Dean. But time went on and there was no action or announcement until a few months later at the close of a Cabinet meeting, the Interim President, Harold, said that he expected to name the new provost the next day and, looking at me, added, "...and I expect everyone knows who that will be."

The next morning, Harold met me as I was walking between buildings, and with a chagrined look, said, "John, I can't do that." He said he couldn't give a reason but implied, without saying so, that his decision had been overruled. He offered instead a one-year appointment as Associate Vice President for Academic Affairs, with many of the responsibilities that would normally fall under the purview of the provost. He said I could move into a faculty position in the Graduate School at the end of the year if I chose to. Though I had been ambivalent about accepting the provost position in the first place, to be whipsawed like that was, to say the least, disorienting. I asked for time to process my response. In the end, despite mixed feelings, I accepted Harold's invitation with the expectation that I would take a faculty position the following year.[13]

I had earlier agreed to give a series of lectures at a sister university in Paraguay that spring, and to my surprise, Harold announced that he would accompany me. He proposed that, after my lectures, we could do some sightseeing and visit the homes of students from those communities who were studying at Fresno Pacific. Afterward, he would return home while I would go on to a previously arranged consulting visit with Mennonite Brethren in Brazil, who were contemplating the formation of a college.

Harold and I enjoyed each other's company and got on well. We were introduced to a diverse array of people and places; some of the communities were highly developed and modern, such as Asunción in Paraguay and Curitiba in Brazil; others were less developed but interesting, like those in the Chaco.[14] Internet access was predictably sporadic but I managed a successful email download at a guesthouse in Asuncion. In the email, there was an invitation from the President of Friends University in Wichita, Kansas, to interview for the position of Vice President of Academic Affairs. It was a position posting to which I had half-heartedly responded some weeks earlier, but had nearly forgotten about. After reading the email, I was preparing to politely decline the invitation. I was looking forward to my new role as a member of the teaching faculty at Fresno Pacific, and well...Kansas? Really? And Fresno Pacific had begun to feel something like home. When I shared this with Harold that evening in the guest house, he said: "No, John, you need to do this!" He was adamant. He knew Wichita, he said, and it was a great place to live. Further, Friends University had a long history and a great reputation in the state.

Harold's argument was, in the end, persuasive. Almost against my better judgment, I replied to Friends, agreeing to an interview date after my return from South America. The interview went well, and shortly thereafter, I was offered the position. I think it gave Harold considerable satisfaction when, at the end-of-year faculty celebration, he announced (with my permission) that I had, just that day, been named provost at Friends University.[15]

As if to test that decision, only a few days after accepting the position at Friends, I received a phone call from a presidential search committee at a Mennonite-related college in Winnipeg, Manitoba. They were preparing to transition from college to university status and were looking for a president who could guide that process. Would I be available, they asked, to become a candidate? I demurred, pointing out that I had just accepted an appointment at another institution, but, after some conversation, agreed to have them send more detailed information and background material. The materials arrived a couple of days later, and I reviewed them. I found the possibility interesting and possibly, in some ways a good fit, but wrestled with the decision. Had they contacted me earlier, I might have responded differently; however, as things stood, there were too many unknowns that needed to be settled in such a short time. Nor could I in good conscience proceed with a candidacy having just said 'yes' to another institution. (And then there was MaDonna's reaction to the possibility of winter in Winnipeg: "Absolutely not!") A possible presidency at a Canadian university became another of the roads not taken.[16]

The decision to leave Fresno Pacific wasn't easy. We had, almost against expectation, found a place we had begun to call home. It wasn't the home we had left years earlier, nor was it the one we might have idealized as we left Africa, but it had a settled feeling. Fresno, its people, and its places had offered us a bridge into an unexpected world, even if we sometimes struggled to find our place. We had found space in the borderlands; a space between worlds, a space where we could thrive without birthright citizenship.

++++++

[1] A word borrowed from Afrikans.

[2] Karla had been researching college options the previous year while we were still in Botswana. Among the considerations was one in California. I had semi-seriously advised her against that one, saying—mostly in jest—something like "there are lots of crazy people out

there." She eventually settled on a different college, but now here we were in California! Whether or not we fit into the population I had described remains an open question.

[3] The Mennonite Brethren were a subgroup within the larger Mennonite population in Russia, primarily comprising individuals who had become part of the pietistic movements. Other Russian Mennonites followed a different religious, cultural, and historical trajectory altogether.

[4] See usmb.org.

[5] These groups, although they were referred to as "Russian Mennonites," were not part of the Mennonite Brethren movement; those who became "MBs" were a distinct subgroup of Mennonites in Russia.

[6] A light meal that might include zwieback, jelly, cheese, and coffee; usually served late on a Sunday afternoon.

[7] One might argue that this was even more true of those "Russian Mennonites" who were *not* part of the MB movement, who maintained a lifestyle that was in some ways similar to the Amish.

[8] Then, as president of a foundation he had established, he had shepherded the college through some of its early developmental years.

[9] The College, now a university, w.as originally founded as a Bible institute, then became a junior college, before becoming a fully accredited liberal arts college in the 1960s. Master's degrees were added in the mid-1970s. Fresno Pacific College became Fresno Pacific University in 1997.

[10] See: Toews, P., *Mennonite Idealism and Higher Education*. Center for Mennonite Brethren Studies, 1995. The differences were to some extent addressed when, during my tenure, the college achieved university status and the graduate programs were established as the Fresno Pacific Graduate School, with its own faculty governance structure.

[11] California's Central Valley is often described as the breadbasket of America.

[12] A tule fog is a thick ground fog that sometimes settles in California's San Joaquin Valley (i.e. the Central Valley) in late fall and winter; sometimes for days at a time. The name comes from the "tule grass wetlands" (*tulares*) found in the Central Valley.

[13] A search committee was formed for a new provost; my name was in the pool, but for reasons I never understood, I was not among the finalists.

[14] The Chaco was a tropical wilderness area where Mennonites from Russia had settled years ago on land made available to them by the Paraguayan government, which invited them to "tame the wilderness" and generally manage their own affairs. Now there was a network of remote Mennonite towns in several regions of the Chaco.

[15] This was technically incorrect; my title was to be Vice President for Academic Affairs, though my role and responsibilities were similar to those of the provost

[16] It's interesting, though useless, to muse in the spirit of Robert Frost, about roads not taken. While I was at Fresno Pacific, I received "cold calls" inviting me to apply for open positions at two different institutions. One in a highly-ranked college in the Midwest; the other in a well-respected university in Southern California. I said "no" to both. At the time I accepted the position at Friends, I had also been told that I was a top candidate for an opening at another mid-sized university in Southern California. Later, while in Kansas, I was invited to become a candidate for president at a small College which I declined. These all became "roads not taken" and fodder for late-night musings on "what if..."

{ nine }

Kansas Redux

It was mid-August when we loaded our car in Fresno and headed south on Route 99, passing through Bakersfield and Barstow. Then, turning east, we crossed the Mojave before climbing to the Continental Divide. A few days later, leaving Interstate 40 and angling northeast, we were unexpectedly caught up short by the vastness of the sky-dome, stretching over the Texas and Oklahoma parries as far as the eye could see in every direction. It was more than we could swallow in a single gulp. Clearly, we were not in California anymore!

It was late afternoon when we arrived in Wichita. It was hot; temperatures were in the mid-90s. The moving van wouldn't arrive until the next day. We spent the night in a hotel and in the morning drove to our new house on the east side of the city.[1] Had someone told us a year earlier that we'd be setting up housekeeping in Kansas this summer, we would have dismissed it as nonsense. But here we were. The 1500 miles of desert, mountains, and plains through which we'd driven over the last two-and-a-half days made it clear that we had entered a different world. We'd become attached to California—both the people and the land—and as we would discover, the plains of the Midwest and the people who live there were of a different kind. Instead of California's relaxed worldliness and inclusivity, we found in Kansas a kind of groundedness and—even among those who lived in the cities—a strong sense of place and attachment to the land. They thought of themselves as being in the heartland, and they generally believed—with some justification-that people living on either of the two coasts didn't understand or appreciate what they represented and had to offer. Kansans, we found, were invariably friendly and hospitable while still insisting that strangers and outsiders must earn the right to be trusted. We found these differences more intriguing than off-putting. Kansas was, after all, the state in which I had been born and where my forebears had deep roots.

Midwestern Quakers founded Friends University in the late 1800s. Several years earlier, the Christian Churches of Wichita had founded Garfield University, named after recently assassinated President James Garfield, on a parcel of open prairie west of the Arkansas River[2] and the city of Wichita. The Christian Churches began construction of a grand building on the empty prairie that would mark the campus. Unfortunately, their efforts were not sustainable, and within a few years, Garfield University closed, having graduated only one class, and leaving behind only the skeleton of the structure that was to have been the university's landmark. Five years later, the empty, half-finished building on the barren prairie—by then a haven for small animals and owls—was discovered by a well-to-do Quaker businessman, James Davis, from St. Louis. It is said that as Davis wandered through the deserted, half-finished structure, a vision began forming for a Quaker University. Davis purchased the building and surrounding land, donating them to the Kansas Society of Friends (better known as Quakers) on the condition that they raise matching funds to complete the building and open it as Friends University, which they did; formally founding the university in the still unfinished building in 1898. The rest of the story, as they say, is history: Friends University went on to become an anchor of the Wichita landscape and the largest private university in the state of Kansas.

My office, newly renovated, was in a suite on the second floor of the original building—now the administration building: a grand Romanesque structure featuring an imposing 150-foot clock tower.

From my office window, I had a great view of the expansive front lawn and the old oak trees fronting the campus.

My welcome by the president and his administrative team was warm. I had, of course, met them during my campus interview. Still, in the summer (before we moved), the president brought his administrative cabinet—my soon-to-be colleagues—to Fresno Pacific to see me in that setting and to touch base with their counterparts there. I joined them for lunch and then spent a few hours showing them around the Central Valley before they departed for the airport. It was an unnecessary gesture, but one that I appreciated and that gave me a head start in connecting with my new colleagues and also in understanding my new role.

While I found it easy to build relationships and establish a level of rapport with the faculty and staff at Friends, there were times when I sensed a certain reticence and uncertainty about how much to trust this "Californian" (which, of course, I wasn't, really). Kansans, it seemed to me, tended toward "this is how we've been doing it and it worked, so why are we questioning it?" But we found, nonetheless, a kind of mid-western(?) resonance with the university and its people that was satisfying and enjoyable.

Friends had experienced significant growth for more than a decade under the current president and were still riding a crest when I arrived. The University had satellite centers in Topeka and Kansas City, as well as several teaching locations in small towns across the state, offering evening and weekend classes. Compared to the constant budget constraints we had lived under at Fresno Pacific, it was a welcome relief to be at an institution where budgets were not uppermost in everyone's minds. However, the organizational structure had not kept pace with the growth; some faculty members were regularly carrying excessive workloads by teaching evening or weekend classes in addition to their normal teaching load. An accreditation team had warned them, in a visit the previous year, about the need to clarify administrative structures and manage teaching loads for faculty. The faculty had discussed various options in response but had been unable to come to a conclusion.

Among my earliest challenges was to recommend an organizational structure that made sense for the university and would satisfy the accreditors. A couple of months into the semester, the president and I made a visit to a university in a neighboring state with a comparable teaching agenda. We didn't, in the end, adopt their structure, but it crystallized my thinking. On our way back to campus, while waiting for our flight at an airport restaurant, I drew a possible organizational structure on the back of a napkin. With a couple of adjustments, we agreed to propose that structure to the faculty at an upcoming meeting. Our proposal was initially met with lots of questions and some clear resistance. In the end, after many meetings, discussions, explanations, and some additional adjustments, the faculty approved the plan by a comfortable majority, and we proceeded to implement an academic structure[3] that closely resembled the drawing on the back of an airport napkin.

Early on, I reached out to the staff at our regional accreditation body, the Higher Learning Commission (HLC), headquartered in Chicago, to become acquainted and for guidance. I was later invited to join their cadre of consultant evaluators. Consultant evaluators served on visiting accrediting teams and led workshops in Chicago. Working with the HLC was an enjoyable, though sometimes tiring, experience; the opportunity to make connections and work with colleagues from other universities was a highlight.

The Amish community of my family's roots was located less than an hour's drive north of Wichita, spread around the city of Hutchinson in Reno County, including the small town of Yoder[4] to the east. The town, unsurprisingly, took its name from a distant relative of mine. Family connections ran deep in the area. My mother's parents, Eli and Fannie Nisly, were married and had begun raising their family there before, as described in previous chapters, moving to Nowata, Oklahoma. This was where my mother had been born and grown to young adulthood. My father's family, too, had roots in that area. His father, my paternal grandfather, John D. (Yoder), had moved there with his family as an 18-year-old when they left a short-lived Amish community in Mississippi. Three years later, at the age of 21, John moved to Oklahoma, where he courted and married my grandmother, Katie. The two of them moved back to Hutchinson some years later after the rest of their clan left Garnett and moved east.

We drove up to Reno County numerous times, meeting cousins and other relatives, some of whom we'd never met before. We reconnected with my favorite childhood uncle, Dad's youngest and only living brother at the time, now elderly and widowed. We reminisced about the time when, as a young, unmarried man, he had brought his parents (my grandparents) to visit us in Virginia soon after we'd moved there. My uncle had joined a Mennonite church and was therefore able to own a car. My Amish grandparents were happy to ride with him to Virginia.) He had always had a treasure trove of (usually humorous) stories and seemed to genuinely enjoy us as children. Once, when my siblings came to our place in Wichita for a family reunion, the Hutchinson relatives organized a reunion of our extended family, giving us an opportunity to connect with still others.

Visiting Hutch (as the locals called it) and reconnecting with extended family felt like an improbable life arc—returning after a long absence to a place of beginnings—that was both unexpected and hard to explain. I had only been to "Hutch" once before when I was 12 or 13 when I had visited there with my parents, but even the landscape: flat and wide-open, the graveled country roads laid out in compass directions, a cross-road each mile, seemed vaguely familiar—like I'd been there before. Perhaps it was my brain playing tricks, but it was hard to explain the sense of feeling at home" there, decades after my only visit. It was hard to keep from wondering whether some long-dormant, poorly understood memory traces, buried deep in our family's collective psyche, had somehow been re-awakened.

The church was an important part of our Wichita sojourn. We found a welcoming congregation of Mennonites in the city, and both MaDonna and I soon carried leadership roles. Still more important, though, was a small group of friends with whom we met regularly for shared meals and conversation. They had all been "born and bred" in Kansas: college professors, a builder, an aircraft engineer and pilot, a botanist. Several had had significant international experience. Collectively, there seemed to be something of an intangible "Kansas quality"—grounded yet open—about the group with which we felt at home. Calling themselves "the questioners," it was a setting in which no topic or question was off the table; we felt understood.

It was in Wichita that we first encountered the Quakers. Not that we hadn't known of them, of course, but it was in Kansas that we came to know them personally and to understand something of their journey as a Christian religious movement. They, too, had a history of being "in but not of" the people among whom they were living. The history of Quakers in Kansas begins in 1834, when Quakers established a mission to the Shawnee people, Native Americans of Kansas. Other missions to native Americans followed, and Quaker communities spread rapidly across the state in the latter half of the 1800s. With a long history of opposing slavery, Kansas Quakers played important roles in the Underground Railroad, including a "railroad stop" in Wabaunsee County, some 50 miles north of Wichita.

By the time I arrived, Friends University typically described itself as "formerly Quaker." However, there were still elements of that heritage embedded in its "institutional DNA," traditions that harkened back to the University's Quaker roots, such as making decisions by "rules of consensus." (A practice I applauded in principle but found—I thought—barely manageable in a university setting.) We came to respect the Quakers and their grounding belief "there is that of God in every person." We came to understand the Quakers as diverse[5] yet still sharing a common ethos and a certain common culture.[6] While the history and the stories of Quakers and Mennonite Brethren, as we had learned to know them in California, were obviously very different, we found common elements between the two, particularly in their willingness to stand for unpopular principles, which often resulted in their drawing bright lines between themselves and the dominant culture. We gained a deep appreciation for their willingness to be different; for their insistence that all voices deserve to be heard, for their commitment to peace-building, and for speaking truth to power.

But beyond the people and the institutions there seemed to be something uniquely "Kansas" in the land itself that became a part of what we experienced there and we wondered if the people of Kansas had in some ways been shaped by the land they lived in, Some years back a couple of (apparently bored) physicists compared the average relative distance between the "ridges and flat parts" of both Kansas and pancakes and determined that Kansas was, indeed, flatter than a pancake. But though we missed the mountains, we came to love the wide-open spaces. While the vast majority of travelers crossing Kansas, whether by air or by road, seemed to agree that the best way to deal with Kansas was to get over or through it quickly, we found the opposite to be true. We were drawn to the immensity of the open spaces and the variety of plant and animal life that was often hidden from those who didn't take time to look. There was something in the landscape that drew us in, and it wasn't long until, on trips back east, we felt distinctly claustrophobic among the trees and buildings that blocked the horizon.

Kansas, we discovered, wasn't empty. Those who treated it as fly-over country apparently missed its richness. We spent hours "on the land," absorbing, somehow, the seeming human insignificance in prairies that stretched from "sky to sky." We discovered a rich variety of bird and animal life on the prairies, in the wetlands, and in the woodlands. Kansas, we learned, was situated along a major migratory route—a flyway—for many species of waterfowl, songbirds, and raptors. We soon learned about the richest viewing spots and the best times to visit them. Hunkering down on the edge of a large salt marsh at sundown during the migration of Sandhill Cranes was, in the best sense of the word, mind-blowing. We would watch and listen as tens of thousands of these giant birds emerged from the sunset to settle into the safety of open water. It was an experience that will never be forgotten. The Tallgrass Prairie Preserve in the Flint Hills was another favorite where we were mesmerized in a different way. The preserve was vast; more than ten thousand acres of open, rolling prairie where the only trees to be seen marked often-dry stream beds. There were few fences and even fewer people. Instead, there were bison,[7] antelope, jackrabbits, and coyotes. Seasonal wildflowers proliferated, giving lie to the notion of the prairie (and Kansas) as empty space.

And then, of course, there was the Kansas weather—not something to look for, because it just, so to speak, came at you. California friends had warned us about Kansas weather before we moved. Apparently, ignoring California's earthquake zones and proclivity to wildfires, our California friends warned us about tornadoes (remember Dorothy in the *Wizard of Oz*, they said). Furthermore, it was unbearably hot in summer and the wind was bitterly cold in winter. They were, we found, partly right: summers were hot, though the low humidity helped make it bearable, and winters were cold. But summer evenings could be pleasant; we often enjoyed our evening meal on our backyard patio. We learned to adjust expectations: when to go out and when to stay in. The farmers needed dry, hot weather so that their wheat could mature, and we were willing to grant it to them, not that our feelings made any difference, of course.

We did discover—hardly a surprise—that Kansas weather can be changeable! Perhaps the most extreme example was a sunny spring morning with temperatures in the 60-70°F range that, by late afternoon, had morphed into a below-freezing snow and ice storm.

With little protection from natural landforms such as mountains, the winds and weather fronts have free rein to barrel through the state as they please, leaving us to "enjoy" the variety! Despite living in what is known as "Tornado Alley," we never witnessed any active tornadoes during our nine years of residence there. But the threat was real. I was reminded of my mother's stories about how, as a child, she remembered being rushed into the "cave" (a cellar-like space underground, common at that time in that part of the world) when a tornado was spotted coming toward them. Once, when a tree limb fell onto the trapdoor entrance to their cave, they had to wait until a neighbor came by to check and remove it. A few years before we had moved to Wichita, a tornado had ripped through a small town just a few miles to the east, literally leveling whole sections. It was also while we were living in Wichita that the small town of Greensburg, some 125 miles to the west, had been almost completely obliterated by a tornado one spring morning. Ninety-five percent of the town was leveled; ten people were killed, and many more were injured. Driving through the disaster area some weeks later was sobering; we had never seen anything like it. Gratifying, on the other hand, was the tremendous outpouring of assistance that came in many forms from all over the world to help the town and its people recover.

It was during my ninth year at Friends that the president and I began conversations about retirement. We were both about the same age and thus eligible to retire within a similar window. He felt it would be ill-advised for both of us to retire in the same year, so the question became "who goes first?" I hadn't given much thought to retirement scenarios until he raised the question, but he said I should make my decision first. After some weeks of reflection and discussion with MaDonna, I told him I would let him go first; I would stay another year. We announced our plan[8] and the Board of Trustees organized a presidential search. In due course, a new president was selected, but as it turned out, the incoming president wanted to hire his own VPAA, and I was informed that this would be my last year at Friends.

Although I had considered retiring at the end of the year before deciding otherwise, having the matter taken out of my hands was disconcerting. It is, of course, commonplace that new university presidents have the right to choose their own team, but it was hard to keep from feeling devalued. In the end, I announced my retirement as a "change of plans," and enjoyed the retirement celebrations and expressions of appreciation. MaDonna had been working in a special education classroom in the city schools since our move to Wichita, but decided to retire the same year that I did.

Earlier that year, we had made plans for a couple of weeks vacationing in Tuscany, Italy, immediately after the end of the spring term. We had been there before, renting an apartment in an old converted farmhouse on the edge of a small village, and looked forward to returning there. Exploring the Tuscan countryside and taking long evening walks among vineyards and grain fields offered a welcome change of perspective, helping to set the stage for the life changes that retirement would bring.

We had decided to move to Central Maryland, where our son, Daryl, his wife, Sarah, and their twin sons had relocated the previous year: Sarah to a faculty position at the University of Maryland and Daryl to expand his professional opportunities as a singer.[9] We had put our house on the market before leaving for Tuscany, but it didn't sell until late summer. It was in mid-October that we watched the moving van pull away from our house in East Wichita. It had been an unsettled summer, and we were looking forward to a change of location and beginning a new chapter. We finished stuffing last-minute things into the corners of the two cars—loaded to the gills—that we'd be driving east, then made our way to the small house across town where we'd arranged to stay for the weekend. Goodbyes were said, and early on a Monday morning, we, too, headed east toward Catonsville, a suburb of Baltimore. We'd be staying with Daryl and his family until we could find a place near them, we hoped, where we could, once again, settle into a place we could call home. Kansas had been good for us; we had been enriched by the people and by the land, and we pondered the ways in which we had felt unexpectedly connected to both. It was a world that, in ways we somehow couldn't fully understand, had seemed to welcome us in connecting with a grounded present and reconnecting with a more distant past. But now we were once again about to cross borders into another foreign world—but maybe, for all that, it wasn't as foreign as it might have seemed at first. Maybe we had come to something that resembled a full circle.

Retirement is supposed to be relaxing and a kind of ending. After years of tightly scheduled meetings, phone calls to be returned, and a list in my head—never mind the written ones—of things that must be remembered and done, it was a welcome relief to wake up on a morning and realize that I could choose to have a late coffee or mow the lawn. But identity and self-worth are, in our world, often closely entwined with what we do—our vocation or career—and I was no exception. The phone that didn't ring signaled that I was no longer needed. During my working years, I had become convinced—wrongly, of course—that if I shut down, the "world" (well, at least my piece of it) would shut down as well. Now I was out of the action and the world, it seemed, hardly noticed. I was once again entering a new world, one that forced me to reassess the basis of self-worth.

Intellectually, the answer was obvious; emotionally, things happened more slowly. It helped that I didn't immediately step away from all professional activity. I continued as a Consultant Evaluator for the Higher Learning Commission for a couple of seasons, did some consulting for my alma mater in Virginia, made three consulting trips to a university in Kazakhstan as a Fulbright Specialist Fellow, and taught online for a university in the Northwest for some months. An invitation from the Dean of Education[10] at Fresno Pacific to conduct a day-long workshop for their faculty retreat was particularly satisfying. A reception had been organized in my honor, and I was able to reconnect with many of my former colleagues. (The dean, who escorted me around campus, said I was greeted like a rock star. That was dubious to be sure—but to this self-effacing Amish boy, it felt good.)

Retirement ushered me into still another new world—except that in some ways, it wasn't new. Maryland is not Virginia, of course, and Catonsville is clearly not Stuarts Draft, but it was still East Coast and though we hadn't lived in that part of the country for decades, coming to Maryland felt somehow like a return. The sense of having come full circle was inescapable.

++++++

[1] Wichita natives had a way of differentiating between those living in the eastern suburbs and those living in the western ones. Those who lived on the west were called "squinters" because they drove to downtown to work every morning, facing the sun, then repeated the process every afternoon but in reverse. One could tell the squinters, they said, by looking at their eyes, which would have a permanent squint. Our new home was on the east side.

[2] The University would also be located just west of the famous (or infamous) Wichita Stockyards, a major destination for the cattle drives of the mid-to-late 1800s. For a time, the Wichita stockyards were the endpoint for the cattle drives along the Chisholm Trail. The area just west of the stockyards became famous for its saloons and "nightlife" that would please cowboys fresh off the trail who had just gotten paid and had wads of salary to spend.

[3] Key to the proposal was restructuring the academic programs into three schools, each with its own dean, that would be represented by an elected faculty on an academic cabinet. It was a novel idea for

the University and perceived by some as contrary to the Quaker tradition of meetings, where decisions were made by the rules of consensus.

[4] There is a restaurant in Yoder that is well-known as a destination for Amish cuisine. Their cinnamon rolls were as large as a dinner plate.

[5] There were three different strands of Quakers in Wichita: the "unprogrammed" or "Silent" Quakers, an Evangelical group, and a third group that incorporated elements of both. The latter two were represented on the Board of Trustees at Friends.

[6] I once conducted a study on the differences and similarities between Quaker and Mennonite cultures as expressed in higher education. I presented the paper at a conference of Quaker higher education in England.

[7] The bison were a managed herd.

[8] The local paper carried a story about it and called our plan an excellent example of planned leadership transition.

[9] Karla had been living in Washington, D.C., since graduating from college and had been working with non-profit agencies doing international development projects for some years. We were delighted when, a year after our move to Maryland, Rodney, his wife Juliette, and their two children moved from their college teaching positions in New York state to faculty positions at Goucher College, some 20 miles from us.

[10] (My former role no longer existed; Fresno Pacific had, in the interim, adopted a different academic structure.)

{ **ten** }

Epilogue

What we call the beginning is often the end
And to make an end is to make a beginning.
The end is where we start from.

..........and........

We shall not cease from exploration
And the end of all our exploring
Will be to arrive where we started
And know the place for the first time.

From T.S. Eliot: *Little Giddings*

Not unlike the African proverb[1] about finding direction by re-turning to the place of origin or the retelling of intergenerational family stories,[2] Eliot eloquently captures the paradox: beginnings and endings are intertwined. Stories can be linear: each linked to another that comes before or after. But stories can be circular too, encompassing past, present, and future in a repeating circle, where endings become beginnings and beginnings become endings—and where we see both as though for the first time.

It was in Kansas that I began to reflect on what I have since come to believe is a quest shared by many: the search for an authentic identity—asking, who am I, really? What were the "raw materials," so to speak, that went into making me who I am? I wondered how the experiences of my parents and grandparents (and of their parents before them), had shaped them; their sense of who they were and how they told their story. I wondered how much of that culture and worldview, that "cultural and social DNA," had been (much of it unwittingly) "baked into" my own sense of self and my place in the world? How and in what ways were their deeply ingrained values and worldview reflected in my own? I thought I had left that world, the world of my childhood, behind, but I was becoming less sure.

The world in which an Amish boy had tried to find and understand himself years ago no longer existed—nor, for that matter, did that boy. That was, he thought, the boy he had left behind. But there was a sense in which he was still the Amish boy from Stuarts Draft. That identity would be forever a part of who he is. He can forever not be the boy who swam in the creek, who took long walks in the woods with his dog, and who read poetry aloud above the noise of the tractor. He is still the boy whose parents trusted and believed in him and whose family, despite differences, always stood together. That boy is still there. Like Buechner's snail,[3] that's a world and an identity that's attached to his back and that he can't shake off. But that boy carried his world into a lifetime of other worlds, and those worlds changed both the boy, his ways of seeing himself, and the world he lived in. He came to see the world of his origins as though from a distance and as though for the first time. That world no longer looked the same, yet it felt paradoxically familiar.

There were remnants of his upbringing that the boy couldn't escape; that stuck to him like idealistic burrs—regardless of whether or not he still lived by them. They included things such as the Amish virtues of *demut*[4] (a kind of humility that avoids drawing attention to oneself) and *gelassenheit*[5] (translated variously; often taken to mean acceptance of what is; serenity), and a tendency to observe from a distance rather than engage worlds that were outside of his circle. He had been socialized into a world with bright lines between "us" and "them." He had inherited a kind of typical—if not universal—Amish personality:[6] deferential but—outwardly at least—confident in who they are. But other worlds had pulled him in other directions.

The boy had rubbed shoulders and worked alongside colleagues from around the country and around the world, colleagues whose roots were anchored in worlds radically different than his. They accepted him as a colleague and sometimes friend, though they were no doubt puzzled when he didn't seem to know much about the music they had listened to or the movies they had watched as teenagers. He didn't usually share much about his background or his growing-up years; they wouldn't have understood, and there would have been too much to explain. But sometimes he wondered if he was living a double life; a life with one foot in each of two (or more!) worlds—worlds that knew or understood nothing of each other and that even lacked a language with which they could talk to each other. What if, for example, that tall, self-assured Swedish woman, an internationally recognized researcher with whom he sometimes collaborated, knew that he was an Amish farm boy who had never finished high school? Or what if his teammates on a university accreditation visit, who remarked casually about their parents' and siblings' professional or academic achievements, knew that his parents' education had never gone beyond a one-room elementary school? In which world did he really belong? Maybe he didn't fully belong to any of them? Was he in or was he out? Had he become "of" those worlds or had he not? The answer, he began to believe, was "yes"—that in some paradoxical way he was at one and the same time both "of" and "not of" all of them.

To be in a world is to be physically present, of course. Either one is there or it is not. But to be "of" a world is more complicated. For the Amish among whom I grew up, to be "of the world" meant being "worldly"—a word without a clear definition but generally taken to mean dressing and behaving like non-Amish: especially wearing "worldly" clothes, doing "worldly" things, liking "worldly things" and adopting "worldly" values. The Amish *ordnung* (rules) defined the boundaries—the outward ones at least—between them and the "world." But there was also a more subtle distinction that was internal. It had to do with a mindset; with how one saw oneself in relation to the rest of the world—a distinction based on mental constructs that drew the bright lines between "us" (the Amish) and "them" (the non-Amish). It was a distinction maintained by outward appearances, but it was deeper. To be "of the world," as they understood it, was to internalize a particular worldview; a worldview that integrates those thought patterns and behaviors into internalized definitions of one's self and that interprets the world through those eyes. It meant feeling, somehow, that one belonged (or not).

What does it mean, then, to be—as the Amish put it—in a world but not of it? And how does one recognize the boundaries? The answers, if they exist, are complicated. Some boundary lines are bright and clear: one is either in or not in. But others are ambiguous, with fuzzy markers and lines that are unclear. Whether or not one is "in" a world may be clear; whether or not one is "of" that world is less so.

Returning to the places of beginning (mostly figuratively, of course, but there was a literal element too) and seeing them "as though for the first time" has meant discovering that I am who I've always been—even when, in another sense, I'm not. I can no longer claim birthright citizenship in my world of origin; the stream of my life has been irrevocably altered by all the tributaries that have merged with the upstream headwaters. Now that stream both is and isn't the same. Perhaps I've staked out a claim to space between worlds—space in a borderland that exists, somehow, between all of those other worlds. Having left one world but not fully entering another, leaves me in a no-man's land—an unclaimed space between worlds. But others live there too; others who share that space and who find that they too can, at one and the same time, belong and not belong. We've found that we can't live outside of our story. We've learned the contours of our own skin—and have found that it fits. It is, I think, a good place to be.

++++++

[1] See epigraph for Part One.

[2] See my comments in the Preface about where family stories begin and end.

[3] See note and reference in the Preface.

[4] This included being loud or over-exuberant. Any kind of loudness or exuberance would earn a quick reprimand from my mother.

[5] The term doesn't translate well. It was popularized by the thirteenth-century German mystic, Meister Eckhart. He used it to mean "letting go."

[6] The inheritance was, no doubt, both biological and social/cultural. Some of the socialization may even trace its origins back through some 300 years of more or less unbroken Swiss heritage.

John Yoder was born into an Amish family in rural Kansas then, at a young age, moved with his family to an Amish community in Virginia where he grew up. He is retired from a career as a professor, dean and chief academic officer at universities in Africa and several US states. He has traveled widely as a consultant and lecturer including, besides the US, Mexico and South America, Europe, Central Asia and China. He has a bachelors degree from Eastern Mennonite College, and a masters. and a Ph.D. from the University of Virginia. He and his wife now live in a suburb of Baltimore Maryland where they enjoy being near their three children and four grandchildren.

www.ingramcontent.com/pod-product-compliance
Lightning Source LLC
Chambersburg PA
CBHW060526150626
46550CB00020B/1968